I Love My Angel

Front Line War II Infantryman 2nd Louie

Walter C. Cox, Jr.

Library of Congress Control Number: 2013920857
ISBN 978-1-956010-44-2 (paperback)
ISBN 978-1-956010-45-9 (digital)

Copyright © 2021 by Walter C. Cox, Jr.

All rights reserved. No part of this publication may be reproduced, distributed, or transmitted in any form or by any means, including photocopying, recording, or other electronic or mechanical methods without the prior written permission of the publisher. For permission requests, solicit the publisher via the address below.

Rushmore Press LLC
1 800 460 9188
www.rushmorepress.com

Printed in the United States of America

Author Credits

READING THE LIFE OF OUR PRESIDENTS, ESPECIALLY THE GREAT OFFICER, DWIGHT ESENHOWER WAS THE FACTOR IN CREATING THIS BOOK

   I WANT TO THANK MY WIFE PAM & MY FRIEND RYAN MESSNER FOR THE PATIENCE AND ADVICE GIVEN ME DURING THE PREPARATION AND FINAL CORRECTIONS!

Contents

Growing Up during the Depression of the Thirties.................. 1
Learning years 19
Hunting 32
Fun Times.. 35
College Days 41
Army Training 55
Training for Combat 65
Combat France: The Other Battle of the Bulge..................... 71
The Battle is Won... 80
Discharge from the Army..113
New Lawyer...119
A JAGC and Korea... 128
Attorney Second Time Around 141
Married Life and Second Daughter 148
Walter's mom 152
Glen Wallace Cox 158
More of Life and as a Law Partner.. 160
Again thinking back about growing in Lancaster 165
Fast forward to law practice...167
Becky growing 173
Golf with Walter 177

More Golf with Walter and friends	179
Return to the battle fields	185
New abode downtown	190
Trips for hunting	194
Fishing Trips	199
Newly Married	205
1980 New Home in Ft Myers	213
What? A Boy	218
Out of Retirement	227
Religion	234

Growing Up during the Depression of the Thirties

Walter was born November 9, 1922, (PERSONS born in 1922 are Betty White, Eleanor Parker, Cyd Charisse, Redd Fox, Judy Garland Kay Starr and persons born on November 9 are David Duvall, Tom Weiskopf) (on November 9th, the gates to West Berlin were opened by Russia (On November 9, 1930 the first non stop airlines flight from New York to Panama)

1922 WORLD EVENTS: Jan 30-World Law Day lst celebrated. Feb 22 Congress authorizes Grant Memorial $1 gold coin. Feb 27 Supreme Court unanimously upheld 19th amendment giving women the right to vote. Mar 6 Babe Ruth signs 3 years at $52,000 a year with NY Yankees contract Mar 14,15,16 Radio transmissions begin. April 16 Annie Oakley sets women's record by breaking 100 Clay targets in a row. May 23 Walt Disney incorporates his 1st film company. May 19 US Supreme court rules organized baseball is a sport and not a business and not subject to antitrust laws. May 30 Lincoln Memorial dedicated Greece won independence from Turkey.

His parents who were both twenty-two years of age. The birth took place in the Ephraim McDowell Hospital in Danville, Kentucky, where Blanche Marie Phillips, his mother, had lived since 1916. Dad (David) and Viola Phillips, Blanche's father and mother, lived two blocks from the hospital. Walter's parents, Walter Sr. and Blanche, lived in Lancaster, Kentucky and had just bought a new home in Haselden Heights, where they lived until both died. Walter was told that the house was purchased for $1,800 in 1922, when Walter was born. It was a large house with four rooms on the first floor and two bedrooms and a hall on the second floor but no basement. There was no water and only electric bulbs were hanging from the ceiling. A cistern out back was the water supply and a little two-hole house out back served as the alternate to a bathroom. The lot was 50-by-150 feet, backing on to a farm.

As to Walter's mom's mother and father, Dad (David) Phillips was a master barber on Third Street, just behind the Spoonamore Drugstore at the corner of Main and Third streets in Danville, Kentucky. Dad had five barbers besides himself and his chair was the last one in the line. The shop had showers in the rear and almost every man in

Walter age 3

Walter & Papaw Phillips

Danville came to get a shower, shave, shine, or haircut during the day or week.

When Walter Clay was only four or five years of age, he would visit his grandparents during the summer months and Dad would take him to the shop many days during his stay with them in Danville. He would watch the men getting a shave and watch the shoeshine man shine their shoes. Afterward, some of the men would take him to the drugstore and buy him ice cream in a cone. When the day was done, Walter and Papau would walk home and carry the day's take of coins. When they arrive home, they would dump the coins on the table for counting. When there was an Indian Head penny, it would be put aside for Walter and he still has them in storage to pass on to his loved ones. To this day, there exists a one-man barbershop at the same place on Third Street.

When Walter was not up town, he was with his grandmother, Viola. She was an industrious woman who washed all the towels, sheets and other necessities for the barbershop, using an electric washing machine that had a clothes compartment made of copper. It rocked back and forth and sloshed the sheets and towels to clean them. She also had an electric ironing machine, through which she fed the towels and sheets to dry and iron. Grandma Viola also grew a large garden consisting of every vegetable imaginable, a grape arbor, fruit trees and roses and she canned all kinds of vegetables for the winter. However, the main ingredient was wine from the purple grapes that grew in a grape arbor in the rear of their home. The wine (from sweet purple grapes) drew a large number of doctors and lawyers in the afternoon for a glass of the very potent liquor. This was in the 1920s, when prohibition was enforced and there were no cocktail hours at the restaurants.

The one thing Walter remembers about his grandmother was her arthritis. She was always stiff and hurting and as a result, she tried every remedy available to try to cure this malady. One he remembered was a kit that had electrical attachment and clear glass that housed wires that turned red and blue. She would rub those items on her legs and hips, thinking they would help. They never did any good. Every month a black man would travel to her home and cut her toenails and trim her feet. This was interesting to watch and the man told Walter that someday he may wear the winning boxing belt because his uncle Gus Myers who was his mother's half brother was a prizefighter and pretty good.

great grandmother age 96

Walter-Glen-Mama Phillips

One story about Gus was in the news. It seems there was a man who accosted the girls on the street of Danville and the police could not catch the guy. Uncle Gus dressed up as a girl and walked the street where the bad guy had been doing his dirty work. When the man came up behind Uncle Gus, he was coldcocked by the dressed-up Gus and the police had their man. The newspaper carried the story and Uncle Gus became a hero.

Uncle Gus and Aunt Emma, who worked at the Hub Department Store, were living on the same street, only closer to the hospital than his grandparents. They were without children, so Walter Clay was a favorite and was given gifts at Christmas and birthdays. He remembers an outing when his parents, Gus and Emma, took him to Joyland Park in Lexington, Kentucky. He must have been only three years old then and the one thing that sticks in his mind is the little miniature train that he rode on while there. He can remember that because the train had a bell and a conductor, who rode on the engine part of the train. The other favorite gifts at Christmas that were expected every Christmas were *Billy Whiskers* books, which depicted the life of a pet goat and his many antics.

One man (Mr. McDonald) lived only three doors from the grandparents and was a mail carrier who carried mail from the rail station to the post office. Mr. McDonald kept his horse in a stable behind his house and had a buckboard to haul the mail. Every morning at six thirty, he would hook up the horse to the wagon and head out to the railroad station. He would ask Walter Clay if he would like to go with him and being a boy of five years of age, it was a great privilege. He would get up and run to the house at 6:00 a.m. and get on the wagon to sit with Mr. McDonald. Both would then ride the twenty blocks to the station. When they arrive at the station, there would be ten or so large bags of mail waiting to be loaded onto the wagon and Walter would help Mr. McDonald (or so it seemed) to load them. They would then take their bags of mail to the post office downtown and unload everything and then go home and unhook the horse and put him in the stable. This seemed to be the most exciting moment in Walter's life at that particular time.

Another strange part of his grandmother's home was the concrete gutter in front of the house. At his home in Lancaster, there was a dirt ditch that carried water down the street between the sidewalk and the road. This concrete gutter would be wonderful when it rained. The water would flow in large amounts and Walter would make paper boats to float with the water.

Across the street from his grandparents' home, there was an deaf oral school, which exists there to this day. The basketball gym was right on the street and when the boys played basketball, their screeches could all be heard up and down the street. It was an eerie sound and that was so often that he never forgot the sounds that the boys made each afternoon and night.

Centre College is located in Danville and many times he visited the campus and its large trees. The Whisiker family gave the land for Centre and he can remember seeing Ms. W driving a battery automobile that did not turn around. The driver would switch seats to go the opposite way. The old auto had windshields at the front and back. Danville was just cited as one of the ten best cities to live in.

He remembers his dad driving a T-model Ford automobile from Lancaster to Danville, which was about a ten-mile distance; and before the Dix Dam was built, the road ran from Lancaster to Camp Dick Robinson to Danville and crossed Dix River on a covered bridge. Walter would ride in the old open T-model Ford automobile in the rear seat and in the winter, it would be so cold that he would have to be wrapped in a blanket. This trip was taken many Sundays during the early years of Walter's life. There was very little traffic on the roads. Since the old cars had fenders that were flat, in the summer, when it was hot, Walter and Glen would ride on the fenders, holding on to the front lights. Imagine doing that today.

1924 T. Model Ford

When the family arrived back home in Lancaster, the house would be cold, as the fires had to be restarted and rekindled. He can remember that sometimes, it was so cold that his goldfish would almost freeze completely if not for the water around it that was enough to keep it alive. The water in the kitchen was taken from a cistern out back and kept in a bucket in the kitchen, with a dipper in it. Everyone drank from the bucket with the same dipper. Walter was assigned the job of keeping the bucket full of water. He would turn the crank that made the small buckets dip into the water and carry the water until it reached the spicket, where it dumped the water into a bucket. He must have done this a million times during this phase of his life.

When the dam was built, creating Herrington Lake, the old covered bridge, which spanned Dix River, was covered over with the water from the dam as it rose, as were the many homes and all the trees on the area. The area was not cleared before the water rose after being contained by the dam, killing swimmers and fishermen. As he can remember, almost every weekend, there was a drowning in Herrington Lake. A man fell out of a boat and got his clothes caught up in the branches of the trees under the surface of the water, unable to get loose and swim to the surface. His mother would not let him go near the lake because of the fear of him drowning until they built a swimming pool in the lake. All the kids would board a truck with cattle and pay a nickel for the trip to Biggerstaffs, a restaurant with a swimming pool. However, in the rear of the restaurant, there were slot machines just like in Las Vegas. It was known by the authorities, who turned their backs, probably paid off and let it operate.

The old road to Lexington (U.S. 27) was a winding road, especially along the Kentucky River. The road wound around the hills going north and crossed an iron bridge that was very narrow. On the right side, there stood the old covered bridge, which was not used anymore. That wooden covered bridge was known as the largest span of any covered bridge in the United States. The abutments to that bridge are there to be seen to this day. Although the iron bridge is still there, it is closed to vehicle traffic. Going up the hill on the north side of the river, there was one curve that made it impossible to navigate without slowing to almost a stop. When you meet a truck or bus, your car would be in danger of being pushed off the cliff. The cut through was a real innovation for the old Highway 27 and it happened about forty years ago. There is a chimney rock on Kentucky River, just west of the bridge. It could be seen from the top of Highway 27 when Walter was a boy, but now the view is covered by trees. The teacher of Walter's Sunday school class took the boys on a trip to see the chimney rock. It was on a private farm and they left the road and went through dirt roads to get to the site. They climbed down from the top of the cliff to the rock and took pictures.

Walter age 10 on Chimney rock

It would be a great scenic place to visit if it became available to the public.

One event on the street where Walter lived occurred about 1927. It appears that the two men involved lived across the street (haselden heights) at the top of the hill. They got into an argument over the chickens one man was raising and they were in the other man's yard. It ended with a shooting where one was killed. Walter heard the shots and ran into the house. It was a tragic incident and ended up with the shooter going to prison.

Lancaster, Kentucky, was the town in which he grew and grew. It was on a square with a beautiful center, with shrubs and trees and a walkway around it. All the kids in town at one time or another skated around the center of the square. The square's center was torn down in 1938 to make way for Highway 27 to go straight through town as it does today, ruining the look of the town, which should now be returned to its former glory by resurrecting the center.

Lancaster, Ky (The Square)

One Thanksgiving, Walter's dad brought home a live turkey. He also had a large cardboard box and proceeded to cut a hole in the top. Walter was six years old and heavy enough to hold the top down, so his dad asked him to sit on the top of the box while the turkey's head was pulled through the hole. The intention was to cut the head off the turkey and let him stay in the big box as the turkey flopped until it died. About the time Dad started to cut the head off, Walter got panicky and jumped off the box. The turkey got out and since its head was half off, it was bleeding and staggering around. Dad had to catch the turkey and he was really mad at Walter for jumping off the box. Walter never forgot that incident.

During that time, when Walter was seven years old, he tended the garden his dad planted. He cut the weeds and pushed a plow between the rows of corn, tomatoes, beans and other vegetables. During the growing season, Walter would load up his little wagon and go to the neighbors and sell the vegetables. What he sold could be his money for tending the garden. Blanche, Walter's mother, canned vegetables during this time and the entire family benefited from them all winter long.

When fall came, it was time to gather walnuts. The entire family would travel to farms and gather the green walnuts that had fallen from the trees. The hulls had to be removed, so Walter would put them in the gravel driveway for the car to run over them to get the hulls removed. He still had to pull the leftover hulls from the nuts and as a result, the stain from the hulls remained on his hands for weeks after handling the hulls and walnuts. Nevertheless, the family cracked nuts on the fireplace all winter long. Glen Wallace Cox was born March 12, 1926, about three and a half years younger than Walter. He and Walter did not get along too well, as Glen was always following Walter and getting in his way. The age difference was just enough to keep them from being pals. Later, as the teen years came, they were friends and did more things together. Glen was sickly and at night, during a full moon, he would get out of bed and sleepwalk up and down the street in front of the house. He would get out of the house because the doors were never locked and in the early morning, he would go to the house across the street and eat with the neighbors.

From the time he was big enough to run, he was out all day playing in the fields, creeks and streets. If it was not a scooter, skates, or tricycle, it was just plain old walking and running. By the time he was six or seven years old, he had a BB gun and used to shoot at birds. Every Saturday, it was a cowboy movie at the Grand Theater, with all the kids in town. It consisted of a serial, comedy and cowboy movie. As a result of those movies, all he wanted for Christmas was a cowboy suit and cap pistols so he could look like the movie stars Tom Mix or Ken Maynard.

Mom

Walter band uniform

Walter 6th Bday

Christmas was always the best day of the year and before Santa could go to sleep, he and his brother, Glen, were up and downstairs, getting their gifts, which were left unwrapped just like they came out of the sleigh that Santa rode in. Before daylight, some twenty kids up and down the street were out riding their new vehicles, shooting cap pistols and displaying all their Santa toys.

Blanche, his mother, was wonderful and loved to have birthday parties for him and Glen. She loved Christmas and always made candy (fondant with a walnut on top) to give to all the friends, neighbors and relatives. She enjoyed Christmas morning as much as anyone in the world and did everything to make her family feel special. On the night before Christmas, she would take Walter and Glen to the Baptist church and after the Christmas program, all the children would receive a sack full of candy and goodies. Blanche played the piano and then the organ for the church every Sunday until she was unable to do so. She also played for the

Walter with scooter

Walter & Glen

Walter & Glen

silent movies from the time she was sixteen until they started having talking movies. Walter remembers going to Lexington with his mother when he was four years old (1927) to see his first talking movie titled *Danny Boy*.

They traveled by bus to Nicholasville and then rode the interurban (train) to Lexington. They would then board the street cars and go wherever it would go in order to see the entire town. Walter remembers the field stone house on the north side of East Main Street, just before Chinoe Road, where very large houses were built. He always loved to see the stone house and vowed someday to build his own house out of natural limestone rock.

In Lancaster, every Saturday at 10:00 a.m., all the kids in town went to the cowboy movies. It cost a dime and included a serial movie that continued week to week? a cartoon, *Mickey Mouse* or *Donald Duck* and then the cowboy movie. It was a great outlet for the kids and they looked forward to that, just as the kids today look forward to watching TV to see cartoons.

One time when Walter was only eleven years old, he liked the girl down the street who was seventeen years old but was as small as Walter. He asked her to go to a movie with him on a Tuesday night, when the fee was two for $0.25. She went with him and when they walked to the movie, he had to leave her and go to his popcorn stand to get the twenty-five cents. The next weekend, Walter saw her get in a car with an older boy and was jealous over that. That ended his love affair with the seventeen-year-old.

Life in a small town meant freedom to roam, to play, to run and to be your own person. Every day during summer, he along with playmates roamed the town and surrounding areas. A BB gun was important and to shoot birds was the goal. He would shoot little sparrows because he was told to shoot only those types of birds and not to shoot song birds, cardinals, robins, etc. He had a dog named Jake and, later, one named Toughey. They were terriers and would chase cars. They were outdoor dogs and ran around free but would come into the home when he was inside. He also had bird dogs, starting with Jewel, who was bought from a man from near Liberty, Kentucky, for the sum of $50. His dad told the story of going to the owner's cabin, where he lived with three short-haired pointer dogs, all of which were fully registered and bred from champions. The owner had them trained to sit beside him and when he put the food out for them, he would tell them individually to go eat. The remaining ones would sit until he told them to go eat. His dad picked out the bitch named Jewel and paid the man for her and then Jewel's master started to cry. "I cannot take the dog away from you if you are that hurt," said his dad, but the owner replied that he had to have the money and, no matter if it hurt, to let go of Jewel—he had to do so. Walter's dad sent Jewel to be bred to Jacks Blue Willing (a short haired pointer) in St Louis, Missouri and she thereafter gave birth to eight pups. Walter Clay was given the job of seeing to it that each pup received its time at the tits of the mother dog. His dad sold all the pups for $50 each but kept one named Jack.

The dogs were trained to hunt quail and Walter Clay, his dad and the trainer took them to Fort Knox to a field trial and won first place with Jewel. The fun at Fort Knox field trials was to ride the cavalry horses, which were trained to gallop, walk, or run without the rider knowing exactly how to make them do it. One time, Walter was following the dogs on a horse for four hours in the morning session; and when lunch was finished, he was so sore that he could not continue in the afternoon trials. Thereafter, Jack won a first place at Fort Knox. Walter has the trophies and the credentials required to show the dogs were registered.

Thereafter, more pups were born to Jewel and the kennel was quite large at one time. One time, the kennel and all the dogs got sick and Walter and his dad had to doctor them every day. Of the 8 or so dogs in the kennel, three died. The rest of them were sold, except for Jewel and Jack, who stayed at the house until they expired.

Walter Sr. was quite a hunter and quail hunting was his favorite. Fishing was a place for the men to go and drink but after a couple of times coming home drunk, Blanche, Walter Jr.'s mother, told him if he did that one more time, she would leave him and take the two boys with her. According to Walter Jr. and the people around the family, Senior never drank after that.

His Uncle Chester and Aunt Minerva owned a local grocery store on the Square in Lancaster, Kentucky. Walter would be sent by his mother to get groceries. He would ride his bike with a basket hooked on to the handle bars. She would make a list and give Walter a $1 bill to pay. The employees at the store would fill the order from the list, put the items in a brown bag and tie the top with a twine and Walter could put it in his basket and ride home. Incidentally, the employees would wait on the public by filling orders. The canned goods and boxes were stacked on the walls as high as the ceiling. If an item was located too high, they would take a pole with a hook on the end and tilt it until it fell and then catch the item as it fell. One time, Walter and his mother were in the store and the meat was stored in a refrigerated display case just as they are now. There were some large round red pieces of meat and Walter asked his mother what they were. She was embarrassed but answered that they were testicles from calves. She bought one and cooked it and Walter ate it and liked it. They are usually called "lamb fries."

In 1929, Walter's mom and dad left him and his brother to go to the derby in Louisville. A horse named Clyde Van Duesen won the derby. When his parents came home, they had a new car and his mom had a new fur coat and diamond ring. It seems that Walter Sr. had bet on that horse in the winner book when the 500 horses were nominated for the derby, which is six months before the derby. As you know, the odds are large; and when one of the slowest derbies takes place and your horse wins, the payoff is very large. Walter always regretted not asking his dad how much money he actually won.

The year 1933 was about the worst Walter would ever have medically speaking. He came down with the mumps. His jaws swelled almost double, but that was not the bad part. After about a week, his testicles swelled three times their normal size. This lasted for about two weeks and it was painful and uncomfortable. He was told it might make him sterile and that took its toll on his future as a man. Some of his friends laughed at him and kidded him about that. It ended up with one good one and one that never recovered but remained small. However, it never stopped him from producing three kids.

Learning Years

When Walter Clay was eleven, he was told by his dad that he was now a man and that he had to work for a living. He was told that he must from that time forward pay for his spending money, clothes and other miscellaneous things. He was told that he could work for his dad or he could work for himself. Upon inquiry as to how he could work for himself, he was told he could buy a popcorn machine and sell popcorn at various functions in town and on the street at the Lancaster Square on Saturday. This was in 1933-34, during the depression and the popcorn machine and supplies cost $200, which was paid for by his dad with the provision that the money would be paid back out of the first profit. Walter Clay sold popcorn at the softball games which were played at the Lancaster school football field. The use of a little building was arranged for by his father and the fellow that owned it also sold hotdogs and candy. During the summer months, he would make $75 profit each month. Walter was asked by his dad if he knew how much Mr. Gadberry, a next-door neighbor, was making as a teller in the Garrard Bank of Lancaster, Kentucky. Of course he did not know, so his father told Walter that he was making the same amount of money that Mr. Gadberry was making per month. All day on Saturday in the square in Lancaster, he would sell popcorn from 11:00 a.m.

until 11:00 p.m., grossing about $5. Popcorn sold for five cents a cellophane cone or ten cents for a box; therefore, he had to sell over a hundred cones to make the $5. He figured the popcorn cost one cent, so he made four cents for every cone. He also sold peanuts for a nickel a small bag. Walter repaid his father the $200 the first summer. Walter was determined to pay back his loan and to begin building his savings. By the time he was ready for college, the bank account he had established at the National Bank grew to $1,500, even after paying for his dates, clothes and spending money.

On Derby Day, Walter would prepare the names of derby horses in little plastic capsules and go around to the stores and sell each horse capsule for $1. He told the buyers of the horses in the capsule that he would keep only $1 and the balance would go to the winner. After the race was over at six thirty in the afternoon, Walter would deliver to the winner his money. This went on for many years until Walter went off to college. Sometimes he would sell several groups of chances for the derby and make three or four dollars each derby, which was equivalent to $50 today.

In the summer of 1931 walter found a job at some farms near Lancaster cutting tobacco. At 6:00 in the morning he had to be up town near the center where the truck hauling a flat bed trailer would pick up all the men and Walter. They would be taken to the fields where some of them would be cutting the tobacco stalks, some would be stacking the plants, some would be hauling them to the barn and some would be hanging them in the barn sometimes as high as 50 feet. The temperature would reach 100 or more each day and one day Walter became so hot that his head was pounding and he had to quit. The men put him under a tree and gave him water and after an hour he was OK. This employment went on all week and on Saturday, the farmer would pay everyone $5.00 for the five days work.

On one occasion in the spring of 1933, he and several of his friends were going to Dix River for a swim. They had no swim gear, so they went in nude. The river was rapid and Walter got caught in the current and was being carried away. Not being able to swim would have drowned him, except for the help of his friend, the son of the Baptist minister, Billy Gabbert, his classmate at school. Billy could swim a little and he grabbed Walter's hand and pulled him to shore. Whew! The angel. Billy went on to medical school and became a pediatrician. He practices at Owensboro, Kentucky.

At age fourteen, Walter started driving the old 1929 Chevrolet vanlike truck. It was stick-shift and was hard to learn, but a field was the teaching area and he finally got the hang of letting out the clutch just enough for the gears to take over and gradually learned to master the technique. His dad somehow obtained a driver's license for him when he was only fifteen years of age and let him drive the new 1938 Dodge, which was purchased for his mother. In the year 1934, Dad Phillips, the barber and grandfather (mother's dad), died; and in 1937, Grandmother Phillips moved into Walter's home in Lancaster. She had been his favorite and he was glad to have her with the family.

The summer of 1936 was at the record-setting hot temp of 104 degrees and it set records by being that way for over thirty days' duration. It was so hot that the entire family slept on the front porch, in the breeze. The record stands to this day.

Walter & 38 Dodge

His mother had never driven a car and when the family bought the 1938 four-door Dodge, she learned to drive with Walter as her teacher. One day, when she was taking a lesson with Walter, she started to turn around at the bottom of the hill and did not turn enough and ran into a tree. The car had a large bumper and it was bent but nothing else was damaged. The car was black and shiny. It had no frills, not even a heater or radio. His dad paid $600 for the car. Walter was allowed to drive it and one night, while on a date with two other boys, he let one of them drive the car. They were going to pick up dates in another town and were hurrying and did not make the forty-five-degree curve and the car hit gravel, skidded into an embankment and turned over. No one was hurt (his angel was at work), but he had to ask his dad to send a wrecker for the car. His dad asked if anyone was hurt and then came to get them. He was told to never let anyone drive his car from then on. However with $50.00 deductible insurance, Walter had to pay for the damage. No wrecks occurred after that and in fact, none has ever occurred during all these years. An angel is still at work.

The 1929 Chevrolet was bought so his dad could sell refrigerators to farmers who did not have electricity. The refrigerators were very small, like the modern bar refrigerators and was named "icy ball." Walter and his dad would deliver the icy ball in the truck and unload it and show the buyers how to make ice cream, ice and keep items cold. It had a ball on the outside and one on the inside. Freon was heated on the outside by a small kerosene heater and the Freon traveled to the inside and cooled the ball on the inside and froze ice and kept the cabinet cold. It was necessary to light the fire every five hours in order for the cooling process to continue to keep the inside cool. The cost of the refrigerator was $100 and many of them were sold by his dad all over the county. With the rural electric, which came a few years later and extended electric to farms, the icy ball business dried up.

Walter's father, Walter Clay Cox Sr., was the first person in Lancaster to become a radio technician. He attended a school in Lexington on how to fix radios and from the time he was twenty years of age, he was the town radio repair person. Walter would never forget the supply of tubes that his father kept on hand to replace the old-fashioned radios. One time, when Walter was in the third grade and the class at Lancaster School were listening to the Walter Damrosh classical music hour, the radio stopped functioning. Walter's dad was called to repair the radio and he was proud when his dad came immediately to the school and the radio started working after a small tube was installed in the radio.

One of the stories about Walter Sr. was his business of renting taxis. It seems that the T-model Ford auto was the type he rented. There was a counter on the wheel that kept account of the number of miles the renter drove and the fee was based on the number of miles recorded on the meter. One guy thought he was smart and jacked up the wheel and ran it backward, thinking it would take off the number of miles; but in fact, the counter counted numbers both driving forward and backward and the guy had to pay double. His dad, in addition to selling appliances, had a pool room with five pool tables and a fast-food restaurant in front. The food was chili dogs, hot dogs, ham and cheese sandwiches and canned soup. Tomato catsup and mustard were kept on the counter and one time, Walter witnessed a guy just turning up a bottle of catsup and drinking it all in one swallow. In 1933, when Roosevelt was elected president, the Congress voted the liquor and beer to be legal. His dad sold beer at the pool room. Walter remembers that the first day beer was being sold, men lined up at the fast-food part of the pool room and drank beer all day long.

Walter Sr. also had another business, somewhat like bowling consisting of duck pins, only that it uses smaller balls and shorter distances. It was a great treat for the farmers to come to town and bowl. Young boys were hired to reset the pins after they were knocked down. The boys would set the pins and then climb up above the pins and wait for the ball to come down the alley and hit the pins. They would then hop down and reset the pins. On Saturday nights, the entire town was full with everyone in the county attending the Saturday night get-together. The business was best until 11:00 p.m., when everything in the town closed down. The favorite thing for Walter to do while selling popcorn on the street was to watch the teenagers from the country farms. The girls would start walking around the square and after two or three rounds, the boys would start walking behind them. There would usually be two girls and then two boys. Soon they would split up and join each other and continue walking around the square until dark. After dark, they would find an unlocked car, get in the back seat and neck.

One of the major winter attractions was the occasions with snow on the ground and the city would stop traffic on Richmond Street and build a bonfire at the top of the hill for sleigh riding. All the kids in town would bring their sleds and slide down the hill, which was about 400 yards. Someone with a truck with chains on the tires would have ropes dragging off the back and the kids would hang on to the ropes and be hauled back up the hill. After warming a little at the bonfire, it was back down the hill again. What fun!

When Walter was eight years old and wanted a bicycle, there was a boy who was going off to college and wanted to sell his Elgin bicycle. His dad took Walter and his piggy bank in the truck and went to see the owner. The price was $8 and all Walter had in the bank was $7 in pennies, dimes and nickels. This was before the popcorn business, when Walter made that money by selling fruit and vegetables from the garden he helped tend. He also made money (twenty cents a week) carrying in coal and cutting kindling for starting fires. For one year, he contracted to do that for the Van Winkle family who lived two doors up the street. After much talk, the seller agreed to accept the $7 and Walter owned a bicycle. It had a twenty-eight-inch frame and was so high that Walter had to reach the pedals by sliding from side to side, but he learned to ride it and used it until he went to college.

Another favorite in his room was a goldfish. It was in a bowl about twelve inches in diameter and eight inches high. It never stopped swimming; however, it was so cold one winter that when Walter got out of bed one morning, he looked at his goldfish and it was almost frozen all the way if not for the water around it, which was too little that it could barely move. It had been placed by the window, so Walter took it to the fireplace to thaw and melt the ice. That goldfish lived for three or four years and now he cannot get a goldfish to live for over two months.

In 1936, when Walter was thirteen or fourteen years of age, the summer weather was something to remember. It was 100 degrees every day for a month. The dust blowing in from Kansas and Missouri was so bad that people could not breathe. His mother was fussing all the time about dust in the house because the windows had to stay open for the heat. The family slept on the front porch for many nights, as it was too hot in the house. They brought cattle from the West on train cattle cars and when they arrived in Lancaster, they turned them loose. Men rode horses to take them down to Danville Pike to the river. Walter says he can still hear them mooing and running to the water. It was like the Wild West as depicted in Western movies.

Another time, Walter was asked to go along with five men, including his dad, to the Latonia race track near Cincinnati. When noon came, they stopped at the DX Restaurant and had a table full of chicken, mashed potatoes, peas and salad. While they were eating, the owner came over to the table and told all of them that he had a horse running in the races that afternoon. Its name was First Try. That afternoon, Walter was given $6 and told to go bet on First Try to win. The place and show would be $2 each bet or $6 total. Now, at that time, men were making $1 a day, so $6 was a lot of money. Walter made the bet (back then, kids could place a bet). The horse won and Walter pocketed $78. Believe me, he was rich. For the rest of the day, he kept his hand in his pocket around those bills so he would not lose them. The next morning, he went to the bank and deposited the entire $78.

On another trip with the men, in a four-door auto, Walter was sitting in the backseat, next to the left rear door. Somehow he reached to roll down the window but opened the door instead. The door opened back and the wind blew it straight back against the fender and it was a miracle that Walter was not pulled out of the car (no seat belts at that time). Angel!

When Walter was fourteen years of age, his dad asked him if he would like to paint the outside of their home. He was to be paid $25 and his dad bought paint and a ladder. Walter had to paint the house with three coats because his dad had him paint it with aluminum for the first coat and then white paint would not stick on the first coat, so another coat had to be made to finish the job. After that completed job, Walter was asked if he would paint grandmother Cox's house on Stanford Street. Of course he did, with another $25 being paid for the job. There were many fancy trimmings on the front porch and around the corners of the house and they were hard to reach and paint, but he put two coats on the entire house. While painting above a window one afternoon, the ladder slipped and fell through a window. Walter was not hurt and Dad fixed it without any criticism. After that paint job, the next was the Phillips (grandparents) home in Danville.

On Sunday, his dad asked him to go with him in his car. They drove down Maple Avenue, where he was shown a large home with four columns and he was asked, "Do you know who lives here?" No was the answer and then he was told it was lawyer, Green Clay Walker, who had been County Judge, County Attorney and an attorney. They drove on down the same street and saw another four-column home. He was asked the same question. He was told that H. Clay Kaufman lived there and he was a lawyer in Lancaster. On to another street and another four-column home, with the same question. The answer was "Henry Clay Cox, my cousin who is now County Attorney." On down two more streets with a small home on each. The question was put to Walter again and the answer was "Our doctors." The next question by his dad was "Now what do you want to be?" and he answered, "It looks like the lawyers make all the money, so I will be a lawyer."

Walter never thought of any other vocation after that and when he went to college, it was for the purpose of becoming a lawyer.

One Sunday, the family went down to Dix River, to a swimming hole used by a lot of the locals. His dad had several blown up inner tubes (tires had inner tubes blown up inside tires to keep them inflated). His dad stripped down to his underwear. His mom had a bathing suit and brother Glen and he were in shorts. It was great to be with the entire family because that had never happened before. Either his dad would be working and he would be with his mom or, at other times, he would be working with his dad. His mom prepared breakfast for him and his brother, Glen, to get them off to school and his dad slept until after that, so he was never seen in the presence of his mother, except at dinner every evening. Dad would come in about 6:00 p.m. and dinner would be ready by 6:30 p.m. All of the family ate together five nights a week. Saturday night was work night for Dad until 12:00 p.m. and Sunday was with one or the other grandparents.

On some days, the family would drive (ten miles) to Danville, Kentucky and have dinner with David and Viola Phillips (his mother's parents). On some Sundays, all of the Cox family would go visit Pendleton and Mary Cox (grandparents on his father's side) and have dinner with Uncle George Cox and Aunt Lillian Cox (wife), Heloise Cox (cousin), Minerva Cox Engle and Chester Engle and four daughters, Frances, Anne, Ruth and Billie Jean. Frances was two months older than Walter, but they were in the same class in school from the kindergarten until graduation.

Uncle Billy was not married but was always there at the home of his grandparents. Uncle Billy was in World War I and had his uniform there in the house, which would be admired by all of them. One time, Walter Clay was taken by Uncle Billy to a pond nearby Grandparent Cox's home on Stanford Street in Lancaster and caught fish for the first time in his life. They were little fish (blue gills) and when fried by Uncle Billy, they were delicious.

Uncle George had a farm nearby and kept cows to milk. He would be milking a cow and he would tell Walter to open his mouth and the next thing that happened was squirting milk in Walters mouth. It tasted very good and from then on, Walter drank almost a gallon of milk every day while he was a home.

Speaking of fishing, several friends and he went to the Dix River and camped on the bank for a couple of days. They had a net to catch fish with. Wearing overalls, they would go into the river, which was only three feet deep and net fish. Two of them would hold the net while Walter would be near the bank, making waves and noise to run the fish into the net. One time, a fish ran up the overall britches leg of Walter and he held on to it. It was a two-pound bass. Another time, while Walter was thrashing about in the water, something else started thrashing and it scared him so much that he ran out of the river. The boys, Hugh White and Pat Cotton, closed in on the fish with the net and pulled the fish out onto the bank. It was a thirty-two-pound catfish, almost as big as the boys themselves. They had skillets and bread to eat with their fish, which they would clean and cook so they could have something to eat. It was great fun and the fish were terrific being fried immediately after being caught. The boys were somewhat like Tom Sawyer, being out on their own and doing the fun things and cooking for themselves.

Hunting

Another great outing would be Sundays with Dad. Loraine Daniels had a large farm out on Crab Orchard Road. He would let Walter and his dad ride the work horses and follow the bird dogs until they would point a covey of birds. His dad would have a shotgun to shoot when the birds flushed but would not shoot the birds out of season because it was illegal. It would teach the dogs to hold the point until he used the word *fetch*, which was the method to train them to go hunt for dead birds.

Around this time frame, Walter remembers going with his dad, taking hemp seed and scattering it along a creek bed on a farm off Crab Orchard Road. This procedure was used to lure doves to that spot so the men in Lancaster could go out on opening day of the dove season and have a great shoot. Walter was given a 410-gauge shotgun and was stationed under a dead tree? and when the doves would land in the tree, they would be shot by Walter. About twenty-five men would surround the field where the doves were feeding and as they would fly in to the fields, the men would shoot them. It was like a war was going on and Walter loved to watch the spectacle. He has enjoyed the sport all his life and each year when the season opens, he goes dove hunting.

During the past few years, Robert Milward has a farm in Scott County and grew sunflowers to attract the doves. On September 1 of each year, the season starts and during that first week, Walter was invited to attend the dove hunt. Bob took him to a stand in a pickup truck to have soft drinks and water and about 2:30 p.m., they all went into the field and got ready for the dove to come and feed. The fun is hearing the many men shoot at one dove and not knock it down. Once in a while, Walter would get a good shot and bring down a bird. The limit of shooting is twelve birds and within a three-hour period, it is very easy to obtain your limit. Some of the birds were just wounded and they moved around on the ground and have to be found. Sometimes you lose the bird because it has hidden in weeds or recovered and flew away. The hunt is fun and only comes once a year, so it something to look forward to.

When Walter was ten years old, he was taken on quail hunts. There you must walk and follow the dogs until they point a covey of quail. Most times, they went to Casey County where the land was free from cultivation and rough with lots of briars. They would walk all morning and when they needed a drink, they would lie down and drink from the fresh creek water. Walter Sr. always told him that the water was clean being up in the mountains, where there was no one or few animals to pollute it. They would stop for a lunch of sardines and crackers or other types of meat that one could eat out of the can. After walking all morning and sitting down on the ground to eat, Walter would have leg cramps and could not get up off the ground. The others would pull him up and he would slowly walk off the cramps. During the army and many other times, Walter had the same cramps in the upper thigh and still has of them to this day.

Fun Times

After the 1938 Dodge was purchased, at the age of sixteen, Walter was allowed to drive it and go on dates. Usually there would be three boys and three girls in the car, but sometime four of each, four in front and four in the back. A date would consist of buying a Coca-Cola for the girls and maybe putting a few nickels in a music nickelodeon for dancing. Many times, the boys would put up twenty cents each and buy *five* gallons of gas and drive a hundred miles from town to town.

All they would do was visit a small restaurant and buy Coke and dance with a jukebox that could be played with a nickel. Most of the night was necking and talking. Sometimes they would go to a movie but not much. Other times, they would go to skating rinks and skate because there was a roller rink in every town.

Mom & Walter

While Walter was driving the 1938 Dodge, which was almost every weekend, the group he ran with would go to some state park such as the Natural Bridge, Cumberland Falls, Mammoth

Cave and others. One such occasion was on the way to the Natural Bridge and there was a one-lane bridge to cross. Walter was on the bridge when another car entered from the other end and neither one stopped, but lo and behold the angel guided Walter past the other car without a scratch. He could not believe it because there could not have been but inches between the cars and the sides of the bridge. There are initials carved in the limestone on top of the bridge created by Walter. HE has visited the bridge many times since then and now goes to the top via the cable which starts at the bottom and carries one to the top over the deep chasms below. The bridge is a very interesting place and the land around it shows it was under water at some time in the history of the land in Kentucky. The lodge is a great place to eat on Sunday after church. They have a buffet that surpasses most buffets in Kentucky.

Lancaster High School was located in a two-story building. Kindergarten was in the basement and elementary grades 1 through 6 was on first floor and grades 7 through 12 were upstairs on the second floor.

The school was built in the early 1900s and at that time, there were no autos, so there was a stable

Ed Morris - Alma, Walter, Helen

out back of the school where those few farmers who sent their kids to school would send them in on a buggy pulled by a horse. The horse would be stabled all day and had to be watered and fed during the time until the return trip home. Walter visited the home of Hugh White out in the country on Buckeye Road and off the main road, on about one-half mile country road that crossed creeks and was very primitive. The buggy would hold three kids up front and a couple in behind the front seat. The horse was named Red and during the trip, he would let go of his breakfast from the rear and the smell would be unbearable.

Walter visited the farm in the summer and experienced the real farm life. He helped hoe the garden, tobacco and corn and wormed the tobacco leaves by pulling the worms off the leaves and crushing them with his shoes. They made cider from apples pulled off the trees and included the worms—all without being washed before the squeezing took place. The apples were put in the hopper on top and a crank was turned that caused the juice to pour out in the vats below. There was a pond where the pigs wallowed in and Hugh and Walter also wallowed in it. The mud would be a foot deep and it would be hard to walk in, but they would try to swim and keep their heads above water. It was an experience Walter never wanted to do again and didn't.

In school, Walter received straight A's until grade 7 and then the numbers started down. However, the lower grades were very easy for him and he even had to memorize the psalms from the Bible for Ms. Jennie, who taught the second grade. The punishment from the teachers was fair and Walter never received any of the punishment, but some of the boys were hit with a ruler on their hands and sent to the cloak room for a time. Some of them were sent to the principal's office, where they received a few blows from a wooden paddle. It seems that most of the boys did not think it was cool to make good grades and therefore, no studying was done. His English teacher, Ms. Anne Conrad took a liking to him and it helped as she called on him to be the reader in class. He can still hear her say, "Make the bells ring." She put him in plays the school put on and he did some acting the sophomore year through the senior year.

He took a class in woodwork and made a small cedar chest, which he still has today and uses to store various birthday, Christmas and Easter cards. Walter and Pam keep and use the cards and recycle them by sending them to each other. He also made a lamp that is still in the house and a sewing table cabinet for his mother. The class was taught by the football coach, who was readily accepted by all the boys. In fact, Billy Gabbert made holders for books to put on the back of the pews at the Baptist church. Everyone thought that was a great project and Walter wished he had helped.

One time, the coach was talking and Walter was grinning. The coach told Walter to take that grin off his face and grabbed him by the hair and lifted him off the floor and shook him. Walter never grinned at the coach again. The coach was so mean that he and the assistant would chase the football players down the football field with blacksnake whips to make them run faster. Walter tried out for football when he was only twelve years old.

He was big for his age; in fact, he was as big as he was ever going to be. Everyone encouraged him to go out for football. The coaches suited him up in a too large uniform, which was old and smelly. They put him in defense; and when Virgil Kinnard, a senior and over six feet tall, came thundering down the field, Walter threw himself at the running quarterback and got kicked in the chest. It hurt so bad that his mother took him to the doctor the next day and although nothing was broken, that was the end of his football career. After that, Walter was a reporter for the school newspaper, keeping a record of the scoring and yards, rushing by the players while the games were being played and other statistics.

During Walter's sixteenth and seventeenth year, he dated a girl by the name of Helen Downey, who lived in Moreland, Kentucky, which was twenty miles from Lancaster. He would go see her on Friday nights, along with some other boys, Virgil (Mickey) Clark, Ed Morris, or others. They would go to Danville, to the movies, or just hang out at a small restaurant and drink Coke and dance. Of course, there was a lot of necking and parking. When Walter would drive home, he would have a difficult time staying awake and would open all windows to let the cold air blow on his face to keep him awake.

When Walter went to UK, Helen went to Eastern to become a teacher. After the first year at UK, Walter told his dad that he wanted to transfer to Eastern to be with Helen. His dad told him he could go but to expect no monetary help from him if he did. Walter did not transfer and the era of Helen was gone.

The senior play at Lancaster High School was about a lawyer and Walter was the star. He carried a briefcase, wore a hat and had a girlfriend. During the play, he had to kiss the girl (Mary Ruth Wilburn) and they pretended to kiss during practice; but the night of the play, he really kissed her big time and almost got slapped, but she relented. There were other plays where the actors had to go to other cities to compete with other schools. This was the best thing that happened for Walter because it gave him some confidence in speaking and acting before a crowd. Walter was elected president of his class when he was a senior and although the class did nothing, it was an honor. When he graduated, he was one of three boys who went to college. Robert Broadus became a preacher, Billy Gabbert became a doctor and Walter became a lawyer. None of the other boys went to college, although Mickey Clark went with Walter to UK to get a degree in agriculture and left after one day at University of Kentucky.

College Days

Entering the University of Kentucky in 1940 in September, he was seventeen years old since his eighteenth birthday was in November of that year. As a result, he was younger than most of the students and girls, about six months to a year. For your freshman year at UK, you were required to wear a freshman cap and it was necessary to take army ROTC for the first two years. At that time, the land-grant colleges were required to offer two years of compulsory military and two years of advanced volunteer military. The male students were issued a military uniform and had to wear it on campus when military science was being taught, usually three days each week. He learned to shoot rifles, to march, military strategy and first aid. He did well on the shooting range and won a medal for marksmanship, which he wore on the uniform.

All freshmen were required to attend football games and sit in the freshman seats and perform card tricks. The cards were blue on one side and white on the other so that the cards could be used to spell out certain letters. Some signs would be UK and others would be GO CATS, etc. That was a special attraction at games and was really a great gimmick for the fans. The entire stadium, which was Stoll Field, held only 3,000 persons. The stadium was at the corner of Rose Street and Euclid Avenue (now Avenue of Champions). As a comparison to the stadium and games today, it was very small with no lighted scoreboard. Drinking of alcohol was allowed and smoking was not forbidden

Walter took Kentucky History from Tom Clark, a Kentucky historian. Tom wrote the book (Kentucky History) and later became the HISTORIAN FOR THE STATE OF KENTUCKY. He and Tom became friends and eventually they were in the Lexington Kiwanis Club together. Tom composed a history of the year Walter was president of the Lexington Kiwanis Club. Tom died two years ago in 2009 at the age of 101. During the previous year, Walter was at Transylvania College, at a presentation and Tom started back up the aisle toward the back of the auditorium. Walter went to him to help him as he was bent over and using a cane. When Walter asked if he could help, Tom looked up and stated in no uncertain terms, "I guess we can help each other."

Walter took English, math, history, psychology and geology. It was fun and Walter did well with grades during his first year at college. He moved out of the boarding house during the second year and into a room with another student and they took their meals in the restaurant nearby. They would buy a meal ticket for $2 and eat all week. The food was not very good but nourishing and filling. Weekends were hitchhiking home and eating mom's cooking. In 1940 and 1941, all Walter had to do was stand on Nicholasville Road with a bag with UK on it; and within fifteen minutes, someone would stop and ask if he wanted a ride. Most of them were going down Highway 27 through Lancaster and they would give him a ride and let him out at the downtown area of Lancaster. On Sunday, he would get out on the same route and hitch a ride to Lexington, close to Maxwell Street and most were glad to take him close to home. Back then, it was safe and no problem with anyone picking you up to take you to your destination.

The sophomore year, Walter was recruited for a social fraternity (Alpha Sigma Phi). The frat house was on Maxwell Street, close to Rose Street, but the next year, it was moved to a house beside the Maxwell Street Presbyterian Church. All of the brothers met before school started and painted the outside of the house, white brick with blue shutters. The inside was walls of blue and woodwork in white. It was quite attractive with the frat shingle hanging over the entrance and twenty-six boys living inside. The house had an attic floored and all of them put their beds on the third floor, where there was no heat. When a cold night came and it was impossible to stay there so everyone moved their beds to the bedrooms on the second floor. Very little sleep that night. One of the brothers was a track manager at the track team and was graduating, so he asked Walter if he would take over and keep the track manager job with the fraternity. It was an

Walter Jim Bill

extracurricular plus for a fraternity, so he became track manager and earned a UK track team sweater for the year.

During the entire time Walter was in college, he arranged his classes so that they were all in the mornings so he could work in the afternoons. He had applied and was employed by Sears Roebuck downtown at the rate of forty cents per hour. His first job was putting prices on incoming merchandise. He kept the job for a year and then was promoted to sales in the hardware department. During his first year in college, he had nothing to wear except the clothes he came to college with. Seeing the other Lexington fraternity boys wearing long plaid jackets, short pegged gabardine slacks, yellow socks, yellow shirts, red and yellow paisley neckties, felt hats and saddle oxford shoes made him decide to visit the best men's store downtown, Graves-Cox and with no money, asked if he could buy an outfit. He did have a job at a store called Sears Roebuck and they verified the job. Graves-Cox gave him a $35 credit that could be paid back at the rate of $3 per week. With that money, he was able to buy an entire outfit consisting of shoes, socks, pants, shirt, tie, jacket, short beige raincoat and hat. The pants were pegged and were cut short so the yellow socks would show. A yellow tie, pale yellow shirt, paisley red and yellow tie, sport jacket that was plaid and a hat with a brim that turned up at the back and down all around the rest of the brim. At this point in his life, he now was one of the best-dressed fraternity men. He could only wear it when he was not in military uniform. By the way, shirts were laundered for ten cents each.

The first year Walter was a member of the fraternity, the upper classmen would paddle the new members or pledges for any reason or opportunity they could find. The paddle was a substantial paddle and Walter did not have much padding on his hind side. When that paddle hit, it stung like a fire had been lit back there. He made it known to the upper classmen that they must have a good reason for paddling him or they would suffer for it. After that, very few licks ever landed on Walter's derriere.

During the first year, there was a dinner dance held by the fraternity at the Lafayette Hotel. The hotel was purchased by Garvice Kinkead and made into the hqs of an Insurance co. When the insurance company built what is now the Central Bank and Trust co. the building became the Lexington City Hall. It remains the City hall to this date. To get back to the dance, the men wore tuxedos and the girls wore long evening dresses. Walter bought a tuxedo from one of the members who had graduated and was the same size. The price was $25 and that was hard to get in those days, but Walter managed to work enough to pay for it. He invited a girl named Piggie Sandidge, from Stanford, Kentucky, whom he had dated the summer before and she accepted. Walter had to hitchhike to Lancaster to borrow his parents' 38 Dodge. He drove to Stanford the afternoon of the dance and drove them both to Lexington. The dinner served was unusual because the first thing served was a shrimp cocktail. It was served on a small stemmed crystal dish with tomato cocktail sauce in the dish and the shrimp hanging around the edge of the dish. To Walter, they looked raw and he had to watch the other brothers eat them before he would touch one. It looked as if they must be delicious from the way the boys were devouring them, so he took his first bite and from then on was hooked on the shrimp. The dance ended at 1:00 a.m. and Walter and his date were to return to Stanford that night. As usual, the dance was jazz and everyone danced the entire time after the dinner and came out wet through and through.

After the dance was over, they all went to the small hamburger fast-food restaurant where the cost for hamburgers was six for twenty-five cents. The two started to Stanford at about 2:00 a.m. and it was about forty-five miles on a curvy road. About 4:00 a.m., he was so sleepy that they had to stop and sleep for a while. They arrived at Piggie's home at about 7:00 a.m. in their formal attire. Walter went home and slept all that day and swore never to have a date out of Lexington from then on.

During this time in college, Walter learned to dance and the jutter bug was the favorite dance routine. Dances were held in the Ballroom of the Student Union Building at the corner of Lime and Euclid. The dances were held from 9:00 until 1:00 and there was only one break aat 10:30. No one sat down as there were no tables and chairs. All danced and since there were so few girls, there was a lot of cutting in when the dances were going on. Some girls would have 10 boys waiting to dance with them. One girl, Sue Fan Gooding was a wonderful dancer and everyone wanted to cut in on her. The bands were the great bands of that era, Glen Miller, Stan Kenton, Cab Calloway, Tommy Barnett and others of that era.

The first year, he was driven to college with Mom and Dad and was housed in a private home owned and operated by Ms. Costello. It was located on South Limestone across from the Good Samaritan Hospital. There were four bedrooms with two boys to a room and the cost of the room and three meals a day was $24 per month. The meals were not the best, but a lot of potatoes, beans, cornbread, cereal and juice but they were not that bad. All of the boys ran to the house at lunch so they could get their plates filled.

Ms. Costello was the landlady and every time he drives by the house, he thinks about those days. One of the tenants was a graduate and in postgraduate training, so he was looked up to by all the others as if he were a professor. He taught all of the others a lot about how to clean up the bathroom after using it, how to shave, how to get to the table to get food before it was gone, how to make a bed, how to study and other good tidbits.

College was not too hard and Walter took every course for pre-law, as he knew he was going to be a lawyer. Physics, geology, psychology, sociology, geometry, speech, English, astronomy, history, science, trigonometry and among others, military. At that time, two years of college was required before being admitted into law school; and by June 1942, he was admitted to summer school at the Law College. There were only forty law students in school and it was fairly easy, so he kept on working in Lexington and did not go home for the summer. He had gone home the first-year summer of 1941 and his dad had put him to work digging post holes on the farm, mixing concrete for a filling station, cutting grass, plowing a garden and cutting tobacco; therefore, he said he was never going home again for the summer.

World War Begins. December 7, 1941—Japanese Pearl Harbor. The Sunday morning of December 7 was, as usual, a time to rest and Walter slept late. When he came down to breakfast, the brothers, including Jim Rose, were listening to the radio. They told Walter that Pearl Harbor had been bombed. Walter ask where that was and of course, they said it was in Hawaii. All of them were shocked and extremely mad about the bombing, so after Christmas of that year, 1941, at least one-half of the thirty boys in the fraternity house had gone home and joined the navy or army. There were not enough brothers to keep the house and pay the rent, so the entire fraternity moved into an apartment. Walter was elected president of the fraternity and had to keep the chapter books and try to hold it together.

The first summer in law school, Walter landed a job waiting tables in the evening for the Delta Xi women's sorority. It was a plush job at the house on Maxwell Street, only a few doors from the fraternity apartment, which was also on East Maxwell Street, only five houses East of Limestone. The cook was a black lady who befriended Walter and fixed his lunch for the following day and of course, he had dinner at the sorority house every evening after waiting tables for the girls. During the summer, the girls took a weekend off and rented a cottage at Herrington Lake. They invited Walter to go along and said he could sleep on the porch. It was a great weekend; however, Walter stayed out in the sun and received a bad sunburn. What a shame!

After telling all this about college, it occurred to him that he forgot to tell about the Big Name Bands that came to the campus and were playing at the Student Union Ballroom. There were Glen Miller, Charley Barnett, Cab Calloway and many others. The student body was about three-fourths boys and one-fourth girls, so it was very hard to get dates. You would have to ask for a date weeks in advance and then sometime it was too late. As a late-minute date, you could get the girls at Henry Clay High School. The dances were from 9:00 p.m. until midnight and with one fifteen—or thirty-minute intermission. There were no tables and dances were continuous for that period of time. Many went without dates, so they would cut in on the good dancers. Many of the girls would have ten guys lined up to cut in. You could dance one minute and get cut and then go to another girl and stand in line. The men wore tuxedos and the girls wore evening dresses. By midnight, their clothes were all wet with sweat.

There was no drinking of alcohol, no drugs or of anything, except Coca-Cola and water. The only thing to eat was down on the first floor at the sandwich bar. It was fun and it's a shame the college kids cannot have that kind of fun now. College was really interesting because it was small and everyone knew each other. No one had an automobile, except the guys who lived at home and drove the family car on a date. There were a few boys who came from out of state that had cars and one in the fraternity from Connecticut had a 1932 Dodge. He was in great demand

and, in fact, would rent the car to his brothers for a small sum so they could date in a car. Otherwise, on a date, it was walk to the drugstore, to the botanical gardens, or to the fraternity house.

The botanical gardens were a great place to hide and neck; however, the college police would come and shine their flashlights and run them out. If the girls lived in the dormitory, they had to be in by 9:00 p.m. on weekdays and midnight on Saturday. The best of all the world would be some nights when your date (who lived in a dormitory) stayed with a local girl at her home and they could stay out late.

His friend, Dick Naylor, had a car because he had a paper route that went to Versailles and Midway and back home. On Saturday night, the two of them would pick up the Sunday paper at 2:00 p.m. and deliver it by 4:00 p.m. with their girls in the car. The papers would fill the entire backseat and trunk, so all four had to ride up front until half of the papers were delivered. Some of the people on the route would leave the back door open so Dick could leave the paper in the house and collect the money from a special place in the kitchen. It was a different world back then when you did not have any crime and theft and would even leave the keys in the cars and never lock the front door to your home. When the papers were delivered, it would be as late as 3:00 a.m., so after that, they would go to the equivalent of McDonald's and have hamburgers that cost six for a quarter (twenty-five cents) and a nickel Coca-Cola. When the girls arrived home, it would be four or five o'clock. Now that was a big night for the college crowd.

Some weekends, when someone had an auto, Walter, Jim Rose and Dick Naylor and dates would drive to High Bridge over in Jessamine County. This was the tallest rail bridge in the United States and it still is used today. They would walk out on the rails of that tall bridge, not knowing when a train would come, but they never had any train come while they were out there walking the bridge.

Dick Naylor, Walter's best friend and fraternity brother, was a Lightweight Golden Gloves Kentucky Champion one year. He trained by running from the family farm out on Todds Road all the way to the university, about seven miles. He was studying geology and of course, he talked Walter into taking a course in geology. It was very interesting and he can remember the first field trip when they were taken to Garrard County just across from the Dixie Stock Farm at the corner of Highways 27 and 34. There were two or three hills that apparently turned over during some sort of upheaval in past ages and there were rocks dating back 100,000 years ago, when the land was underwater. They found shells and fossils, which were the basis of the studies of the earth from early times.

Dick went on to become a geologist with Exxon and was sent in 1957 to Libya, where he was instrumental in bringing in hundreds of oil wells. He told Walter about the drilling and the amount of oil that was coming out of that country. There were oil pipes twenty-five inches in diameter, pouring oil continuously into tankers when oil was only $1 a barrel. He took his wife, Avis and a son with him and while they were living in the country, they had another son and two daughters. After Godiafy (the dictator) took over in 1967 and the oil company and Dick's entire family left Libya and came back to England, where he was sent to the North Seas of Norway to drill for oil during the summer. Winter would be so cold that they had to cease drilling and come back in the spring to continue. He told the story about capping the drilling holes deep in the sea and when they came back in the spring, they could locate the old hole and continue drilling.

Dick told the story about the oil rigs that were out there for months and the men did some funny things. One time when Dick was being helicoptered into the rig, he looked down and saw a woman in a bathing suit. Upon landing, he found out the men had a balloon woman in order to fool everyone coming in on a plane. After his duty was over in Norway, where his family were living, his oldest son decided to stay and he is there to this day. The rest of the family came back to Lexington and T. J. Moses and Walter, who were in the real-estate business, found Dick and Avis a home at Greenbriar golf course and his wife, Avis, lives there today. Walter, T. J. Moses and Dick played golf at the Greenbriar, Lexington Country Club and Spring Valley golf courses almost every month. Both Dick and T. J. are now gone, with cancer and Parkinson's taking their toll.

College life was different back in the 1940s, as there were only 3,500 kids in the University of Kentucky and they all knew each other. There were no cars except for the kids who lived in town and used the family car. Students walked to all classes, which were all on the main campus, from Limestone to Rose streets and from

Euclid to Cooper Drive. The football games were great and the card tricks done by the freshmen were a sight to behold. The entire freshman class had to report to the stadium one hour before the game and learn how to hold the colors of the cards so they could spell out certain words while the game was in progress. One would have a blue card on one side and white on the other and display whatever word was required to show the other side of the stadium. The law school also had a cheering section and about forty guys would get seats together and do a lot of off-color cheering.

Walter entered law school after only two years of pre-law. In June 1942, there were only forty boys in law school for the summer session. In the fall quarter, that increased to about eighty. He attended three quarters of law school before being taken into the army in April 1943. During this particular time, Walter was elected president of his social fraternity (Alpha Sigma Phi) and Vice President of his legal franternity Phi alpha Delta. His roommate was Donald R. Rose (Jim), who has lived in Lexington since 1954 and owns Carpenter Warren Insurance Agency. Walter was his best man when he married Penny in the Alpha Xi house on Maxwell Street. At the same time, Walter was dating Mary Lee Engle, who lived in the Alpha Gam house just across the street from the Alpha Xi house.

When Walter entered college, the ROTC was required for the first two years for all men. Three days each week, he wore the army uniform and attended classes in military courses. He learned to shoot a rifle, which he already knew and march with the platoons, squads and companies. When the second year was finished, the military was offered to advance ROTC and you had to have good grades and be recommended to get into the third-year ROTC. Walter applied and was approved.

Army Training

During the fall of 1942, he trained to be an officer; however, in April 1943, the entire Junior Advanced ROTC class were required to leave the university, join the army and take basic training and then on to Officer Candidate School at Fort Benning, Georgia. This was in lieu of continuing at college until you were commissioned as a second lieutenant. This event occurred all over the United States at all the land-grant colleges. The government decided it was best to put all the advanced ROTC boys in the army and send them to basic training and then train them at an officer training school. Some went to Fort Knox to be armored officers, some went to the Army Air Corps to be pilots and most went to Fort Benning to be infantry officers.

The training at Camp Wolters, Texas, in the summer of 1943 was the hottest time ever known to him and all the 150 men from UK who were training at the camp. The barracks were buildings with two floors consisting of fifty men each. There were cots with footlockers at the foot of the bed and a small hanging area at the head of the bed to hang the uniforms. No air-conditioning and no cold water for drinking. There was a lot of mutton on the menu and lots of bread, beans, milk and pies. Each morning at six, the soldiers were called to the mess hall to eat and then at six thirty, out in the training ground for calisthenics. The training was tough and soon the fat boys were lean and the lean boys were heavier because it was all muscle. They were on many marches, some five to seven miles, ten miles and up to twenty-six miles. Everyone had to learn to shoot all weapons, learn tactics, run obstacle courses and do KP (kitchen police) duty. There was also guard duty to pull all night long on

Walter on left (After 16 mile March)

some days during the month. Weekends were sat and sun, with nowhere to go and no money to spend. The $50 per month did not take you far.

Walter shot expert in all weapons, ran the obstacle course in fast time and never fell out while marching. During the seventeen weeks of heat, there were times when it was 100 degrees all night long and everyone slept on the bed with Mexicana powder on the sheets because of the heat rash on most of their bodies. The man who slept next to Walter did not get up one morning when called to jump out of bed and he can remember the sergeant named Justo (an Italian self-proclaimed boxing expert) came over and overturned his bed. The soldier came up mad and wanted to fight but he was held away from Justo because he would have been beaten up.

Every day there were calisthenics at 6:30 a.m. and then eat and shave. After that, he and the others were taught to fire every infantry weapon, throw hand grenades, learn tactics, do hand-to-hand combat with each other, run obstacle courses, march, stand guard, do kitchen duty called KP and have a few days where the platoon lieutenant taught basic ways to avoid being killed. KP, or kitchen police, started in the morning at four o'clock. If you were on the roster to be on KP, you would put a towel on your foot locker and the mess sergeant would wake you up and make sure you followed him out of the barracks to the mess hall. You would prepare the mess hall for 200 men who would arise at 6:00 a.m. and come to eat. After that, you would clean all the plates, pans and cups. Next, you would peel potatoes maybe two 100-pound sacks of them, clean the mess hall and get ready for lunch. Again to set the tables for lunch and again get more food ready for dinner, which took place at 6:30 p.m. After you cleaned the hall again, you could go to the barracks and take a shower and go to bed.

On the weekend, they were allowed to go into Fort Worth one or two times during the 17 weeks of basic training. The guys would catch a bus and then and stay at a hotel. It was a great relief to get out of camp and they enjoyed riding the bus into town about forty miles away. They would all go to the USO, which was attended by the girls of the city. The girls would sit and talk or dance with the soldiers and provide some different entertainment, of which they had none at camp. Some farmers from Weatherford, Texas, which was only ten miles away would invite the boys to eat Sunday dinner. One time, Walter went with others to a farm home and found it was air conditioned by a fan pulling air through straw that was wet from a hose dripping water into the straw. The homemade affair cooled the house down at least ten degrees. The food was wonderful at these farm houses and the fellows welcomed the farmers to invite them again and again.

About the time, Walter found out the real truth about being in the infantry; seeing that his brother Glen would soon be drafted, he decided to tell Glen to join the navy. He felt that being on a ship where good food and a dry place to sleep would surpass the bad food and a foxhole. Glen did, in fact, join the navy when he was eighteen years of age and, after training at boot camp, was assigned to the USS Panamint. The ship was a command ship and as a result of admirals being aboard, it was protected from being in combat and usually was in the middle of the armada of ships.

During that seventeen weeks of training, which made men strong, muscular and almost able to do anything. Walter has said many times that all graduating seniors and all boys aged eighteen should have to take basic training. It would prepare them for the coming world, whether it be college, profession, or plain old labor job.

When September came, they were ready to leave for Fort Benning. After being interviewed by a general (the general was making small talk), Walter was asked what brand of Kentucky bourbon he liked. Walter had seen billboards with the name of Old Taylor on them, so he replied, "Old Taylor, sir." Walter had never even smelled bourbon.

It was ordered that the entire company of the University of Kentucky men return to the University of Kentucky because they did not have enough room at Fort Benning for all the college ROTC boys. Walter and the G company, as it was called, were sent by train to Columbus Ohio to Ohio State University, on the way to Lexington. The ride was on an old passenger train that was so dirty that when they arrived, their khaki uniforms were black. They were on the train for three days and slept on the seats, on the floor and on barracks bags. One car was the kitchen and when it would be sidelined to let other more important trains go by, they would eat the slop they prepared on that kitchen car.

When they arrived at Ohio State, they all went to a restaurant to eat some good food. Most everyone had their uniforms washed by the cleaners and slept in the Ohio State dormitories, which were underneath the football stadium. They trained a couple of days by marching on the football field and ran around the field for exercise. Somehow, a sergeant from Lancaster saw Walter's name on the roster and called him in to talk. Bruce Lawson, the sergeant, was an older friend and he appointed Walter to be in charge of the entire company on the train ride to Lexington. Walter had to march the company to the train and get them seated for the first trip to Cincinnati and when they arrived in Cincy, the Company had to change trains and had to march across the entire RR station to the next train. What a challenge to wind in and out with a company of 150 men. After the train arrived in Lexington, the company had to be marched from the Station to an area where the colonel of the post at University of Kentucky was in charge. Walter saluted Colonel Brewer and announced that Company G was all present and accounted for. Colonel Brewer welcomed the company and congratulated all for a job well done. He then stated that they were free from Friday until Monday, when they should report to the University of Kentucky.

Life at the university was to be enrolled in any courses you wanted and help with the ROTC class and the ASTP class in training them to march and other duties. The ASTP group were boys who had good grades and were left out of the draft so that there would be men left from the war who were intelligent. This was great duty and Jim Rose and Walter found a room on Rose Lane for the fall semester. The room had a window opening on the roof of the front porch. It was winter, so the porch was serving as a refrigerator for food and beer. Rose Street was not far from the Maxwell Street sorority houses, so both would visit the Penny, who lived at a sorority house across from Alpha Gamma Delta, where Mary Lee lived. They would stay at the respective houses until they had to be kicked out of the sorority houses. The entire company were under an 8:00 p.m. curfew, so they had to slip around the trees and houses going from the sorority houses to their room on Rose Lane so as not to be caught by the military.

One night, just prior to being shipped to Fort Benning, the two of them, with Mary Lee and Penny, along with several others in Company G decided to go to the nightclub called the Fireplace, which was located on Euclid Avenue. About 10:00 p.m., someone tipped off Colonel Brewer and he came to the nightclub. Someone saw him come in the front door and with the girls' help, the guys all hid in the ladies restroom. Lucky for them, Colonel Brewer did not go there and they were saved from being caught. The next morning at reveille, Colonel Brewer announced that the soldiers who were in the restroom for ladies surely were good at camouflage.

During the time, Walter was taken into the basic training; and during the time off, he dated Mary Lee Engle (who later became his wife). They corresponded all that time and now that they both were in the university, they were together every day. One time, when Tommy Bell and Walter were writing to their girlfriends, Leslie Bruce and Mary Lee, they copied the same poem in their letters. The girls spoke to each other and compared letters and found out about the poems being the same. He was kidded a lot about copying stuff from a book to write to your girl.

When Christmas break came along and Company C was given two weeks leave of absence, December 14 to January 2,

Walter went to London, where Mary Lee was home for the holidays. They went to Corbin to get their blood tests and got married that very same day at the Baptist minister's parsonage, December 20, 1943. Since Mary Lee was only twenty years old at the time, the pastor called her mother and asked if it was agreeable to marry them. She obviously gave her approval and on December 20, 1943, they were married with a couple of cousins as witnesses. Walter had just turned twenty-one on November 9. With no money and very little given to him, they spent their time at Mary Lee's home, except for two days at Cumberland Falls Dupont Lodge. After Christmas, they found a small upstairs apartment on Clay Avenue, which had a small kitchen, bedroom and bath. The entire cost was $24 per month including utilities. It was located close to the university and since Walter had to meet his Company G every morning at 6:30 a.m., after that he would run back home and get in bed and he and Mary Lee had plenty of time to make whoopee.

They received $120 per month of military pay and in order to pay all their bills, they divided cash into various envelopes for the rent, food, entertainment and etc. One time, Mary Lee bought some object to hang on the wall and went over budget and there was a little rife, but that was the only time they had any words. They lived there until April, when the company was sent to Fort Benning, Georgia. Then Walter was gone for seventeen weeks, after which he was commissioned a second lieutenant in the army infantry. During the time Walter attended Fort Benning, Mary Lee went home to London, Kentucky and stayed with her mother. On June 6, Mary Lee's birthday and the day the English and Americans stormed the coast of France, now called D-day, Mary Lee visited Walter at Fort Benning. They stayed at the visitors' barracks, in small rooms with single beds. It was hot, as there was no air conditioning in those days and the mosquitoes nearly ate them alive. They had a great time despite the weather and the bugs. To think about the army storming France across the English channel was beyond belief. Walter was very happy he had not graduated from OCS by then because he probably would have been one of those soldiers trying to climb the cliffs into France.

The time at Benning was fairly easy physically, but mentally, it was tough. Walter hit the books hard and ended up in the upper 10 percent of his class and was company commander the final weeks leading up to the graduation. There was a special event where there would be a display of all the companies training to be officers. There were visiting dignitaries and officers from other countries. Approximately 5,000 soldiers training to be second lieutenants were in the field, along with officers from all the different countries who were in attendance. Questions were asked and candidates were selected to answer the question on a loud speaker so that all 5,000 candidates could hear. One such question was asked, "Over what terrain do soldiers use mortars?" The question was asked of Class 340 and candidate Walter Cox was selected. Walter answered, "Varied, sir!" This was the correct answer and Walter's company commander was elated. He was treated differently from then on until the graduation.

His mom and dad brought Mary Lee to Fort Benning for the graduation which took place August 8, 1944. They drove down to Fort Benning in the 1938 Dodge sedan and then after one day, they all left and drove to Lancaster, Kentucky. For ten days, it was a great reunion. When the couple was in Lancaster, Walter's dad found a 1941 Pontiac Torpedo body two-door automobile for him. Red wheels, blue top and gray halfway down on the body. It was a straight-eight motor and stick shift. The price was $1,400 and was paid for by his dad. During the time following the purchase, it was paid back to Dad at the rate of $50 per month. To have an auto all his own was as close to heaven as he had known. The car was as close to a sports car as he could imagine and loved every day he drove it.

Training for Combat

Mary Lee and Lieutenant Walter motored to Fort Leonard Wood, Missouri, to the Seventieth Infantry Division. On the road to the company location, they observed a major walking along the road. Walter recognized the major as Paul Durbin, who had been on the track team at UK. They exchanged salutes and Paul escorted Walter to his company headquarters, where Walter was assigned to E Co 274 Regiment 70th Infantry Division as an Infantry Platoon Leader of the third platoon.

The two, Mary Lee and Walter, found a room at Rolla, Missouri, with a lady who rented to officers. They had kitchen privileges and a room and a shared bath. It was thirty-five miles from camp and Walter had to be at the camp at six thirty every morning, except Sunday. He came into town three or four nights a week, but it was difficult to train all day and drive in and then drive back out at five in the morning. At the end of the month, they would run out of money; and one time, on a Sunday night, they had twenty-five cents left for food until payday the next day. They walked the two miles downtown to the Blackberry Patch Restaurant, where they ate two hamburgers and then walked back home to save on gas. Walter would carpool and drive his car two times a week and another guy by the name of Wayne Meshier, who was assigned to the First platoon of the same company. Meshier had a convertible Cord 1932 model auto, equipped with a rumble seat. The motor was so loud that you could hear it coming for two miles. It used a lot of gas and the gas had to be obtained from the black-market gas stations by paying more than the regular price and it was all done in cash.

The officers who lived in Rolla, Missouri, would arrive at camp at 6:15 a.m. and stand reveille with the company at 6:30 a.m. The company would then eat breakfast and at 7:30 a.m., be in the field for exercises. They did all kinds of arms, legs, jumps, squats, fingers, head and other types of stand in place exercises. After that, they would have an hour or two of teaching. Walter would teach his platoon of forty plus men, along with the sergeants, who also taught classes. One of the things they had to learn was how to stay alive in combat. It was hand-to-hand combat with a bayonet, with a knife and with a rifle. The idea was to kill the enemy before he killed you. Each person studied all facets of the infantry, so they could shoot every weapon if necessary. Some were assigned to mortars, some to rifles, some to bazookas (a long barrel with a rocket in it to stop tanks, to bring down doors, etc.), some to radio operating and some to ammunition carriers. All had to know each one's assignment. Then there would be field maneuvers and simulated combat, where they would be subjected to these weapons being fired over their heads.

On one such action, the mortar squad made a mistake and fired some short rounds that landed in the middle of a couple of squads of the men. Several of the men were wounded and lo and behold, one landed not twenty feet in front of Walter and did not go off. There he lay on the ground, looking at the mortar round that has a fin to make it fly straight to the target and the fin was sticking up in the air and the shell was buried in mud. Angel on his shoulder. The training was continuous and made the entire division as tough as nails. Walter taught his men the tactics he had learned at Fort Benning officers' training and how to kill the enemy and stay alive. Every day the teaching of his men was aimed at learning how to kill by any method which included hand to hand combat.

On the last day of October 1944, the division was alerted to be shipped to an unknown battlefield. The division General Barnett, came and spoke to the entire division, cautioning all men not to talk about being shipped away from camp. He told the division that he expected every man to be able to stay alive and to see to it that the enemy did not live. It was an explosive delivery and every man in the division was listening when he gave that kind of advice.

Walter begged the company commander, Eugene Sisson, to let him drive Mary Lee back home and after much pleading, he was given two days off to do so. Mary Lee had purchased a cocker spaniel puppy and after loading the Pontiac, they took off and drove all night to Lancaster, Kentucky, where Walter left her and the pup. Walter was so tired that he went to sleep driving and Mary Lee had to do most of the driving from St. Louis to Lancaster, Kentucky. He then took a train back to camp and by November 1, the division was en route to Boston.

Camp Miles Standish was the destination of the and for a few days of preparation and one day in Boston. The only thing Walter remembers is eating lobster and buying Mary Lee a string of pearls. The division boarded a ship (The Mariposa), an Italian cruise ship, with a contingent of hospital personnel and the 274th Regiment, along with General Tom Herren, who was assistant Division Commander. Walter was appointed officer of the ship's main dining room and as such had pretty much the entire affair under his command. The general ordered all officers to dress in dress uniform for the dinner each night, which included nurses who were also officers. The dining area was plush and was a luxury for the officers going to Europe. The food was good and was prepared by the chefs who had been working for the ship before the war.

After the dinner was finished, Walter would take the leftover food from the officers' mess down into the ship's hold where his men were billeted and they would have a feast. The Mariposa was a fast ship therefore, there was no need for protection from submarines. The ship could travel faster than the subs could. It was blackout at night and standing on the fantail was an experience, seeing the phosphorous sparks and the waves from the screw driving the ship. The stars shining and the ship parting the water as it plowed through the waves was a sight to behold. Walter had the run of the ship since he was mess officer and he visited every part down to the engine room and up to the captain's room.

One of the experiences on a ship, for the soldiers with nothing to do but pass the time of day, was shoot dice. The enlisted men did a lot of that and one day, Sergeant Rogers who was his third Platoon squad leader, came to him and asked him to put $3,000 (worth about $40,000 in todays money, in the ships safe. Walter told Rogers that he would comply with one proviso: he could not get any of the money until the ship docked and together they would go buy a money order and send the money home. In a couple of days, Rogers came begging for some money. Walter told him he could not have any money and reminded him of the deal he made when giving the money to him. Eventually, he and Rogers sent the money to Rogers bank. Years later, at a reunion of the soldiers of the Seventieth Infantry Division Association, Rogers thanked Walter for withholding the money and told him that the money was instrumental in getting Rogers through dental school.

Walter left front with platoon

After the ship docked at Marseilles, France, the men were taken to a remote hillside, where they put up their tents and tried to sleep. The area was just dirt and it rained and turned the entire hill into mud. Needless to say, there was little sleep. During the night, a few of his men, including Walter, found a small village close by. Walter and his platoon sergeant, along with a couple of soldiers, visited the village. They also found that the French had plenty of wine to sell and the group had a good time one last night. The regiment was there for four or five days and then they were shipped out by train to the front, starting about December 10, 1944. The transportation was old boxcars capable of holding eight horses and/or forty men. Walter had forty men and they could not lie flat all at one time, so it had to be arranged so that one-half of the men could sleep lying down and one-half would sleep sitting or standing. They would switch about every three or four hours. They had C rations to eat, which required small pans to cook the bacon and other beans. It was hard to do all that in that boxcar and the train would stop at daytime in forests or tunnels because the Germans still had planes flying trying to drop bombs on the Americans. At night was the only time the train moved. During the day, the train would hide in a forest or tunnel and of course, you could get out and move around as long as you were hidden from the sky if a plane came. The French people would welcome the troops and trade wine for food, so the men had little alcohol to keep them going.

Combat France
The Other Battle of the Bulge

On December 24, 1944, the train carrying the 274th Infantry Regiment arrived at the front near Strasbourg, France. Everyone gathered his backpack, which weighed about fifty pounds, his rifle, mess kit, gas mask and other gear and started walking in the snow, which was two feet deep. They walked from about 8:00 p.m. until 1:00 p.m. and arrived at various places just short of the Rhine River, which divided France from Germany. The town of Bischweiller, France, was the destination of the Second Battalion of the 274th Infantry, which was Walter's outfit. After a night sleeping on a concrete floor in an abandoned warehouse, everyone was served breakfast and welcomed the sun, which had not been seen since the start of this unusual trip. There were sounds from the sky and for the first time since the Battle of the Bulge started on December 16, our United States bombers B 17s were coming over their heads in such large numbers that they almost blocked the sunshine. Some say there were 2,000 planes at one time that came over and dropped their bombs. The sound of all those engines was electrifying and the bombs so powerful when dropped that it felt like an earthquake was shaking the ground. During the day (Christmas), his platoon 40 men, all went to church in a little Catholic church that held a maximum of forty or fifty at each service, so it took some time to get everyone in and out. A turkey dinner was served by the kitchen, which had been brought into town and manned by the cooks. The kitchen consisted of stoves which were fired by kerosene and were very efficient. There were 3 stoves and equipment sufficient for the cooks to prepare meals for 200 men in each company. This would be the last prepared meal the men would eat for at least two months.

The post office soldiers brought mail for the first time in two weeks, including packages of food and toiletries. At dusk, they received orders to go to the front line to occupy the foxholes, which the Forty-fifth Division men had been using. At the front, we could see the Germans moving around on the other side of the Rhine River and we were sure they could see us. Once in a while, they would take a shot and we would return fire. The Maginot line built by the French to keep the Germans out of France was along the banks of the river, they were concrete bunkers, which had underground connections with each other and small holes on the German side with which to shoot through. On the other side of the Rhine River was the Seigfried German defense line, where they were occupied by the soldiers of the Hitler army.

Walter was not on the front line but occupied his time riding in a jeep up and down the roads with a machine gun in his lap, making sure no enemy patrols were in the area. Luckily none were encountered and it seemed relatively safe.

This type of light fighting continued until New Year Day 1945 was ushered in with the German SS troops infiltrating through our front lines, one by one in the snow in white uniforms. These troops of the German Army had been in Finland, where the snow was continuous and they were well trained for fighting in woods and mountains. They were the SS troops who captured Wingen-sur-moder (Wingen on the Moder River) located in the Hartz Mountains, France, a little town occupied by the regimental headquarters of the Forty-fifth Division, where much of army supplies were stored. One of the key features of the town was a railroad line running through the village. In the town proper were the Wenk Hotel, the St. Felix Catholic Church and the train station. There were two railroad underpasses going beneath the tracks. The terrain was difficult, with steep slopes surrounding the town. The snow was waist deep, with temperatures around zero and strong winds. The Germans attacked the town at 2:00 A.M. and secured it in two hours. All the prisoners were placed in the church and the nearby houses. All the men of the 45th Division were asleep and it was rather easy for the germans to capture them.

Orders came down for our Second Battalion to board trucks to be trucked back to the town of Wingen, which was at least sixteen kilometers to the rear, to retake the town of Wingen and stop the second battle of the bulge. All night long, their entire battalion consisting of four companies and approximately 800 men were trying hard to drive through snow and ice over mountains to get to the town. It was slow-going and many times, with a wait for the leaders to direct us, Walter and the driver fell asleep and when they would wake up, the trucks they were following were gone. They had to find their way to the truck in front of them, hoping not to run into any enemy. When a cross road was encountered, Walter would get out of the truck and try to follow the tracks of the trucks up front. The battalion finally reached the little village of Petite Pierre, France, where the officers found vacant homes to occupy for the awaiting of dawn and the time to begin the attack.

Early in the morning, the men were told to get ready to retake the town and that there were only a few Germans occupying it. The company moved down a hill into the woods and emerged looking at the town of Wingen. Then a strange thing happened. A German soldier held up a white flag and that meant to Walter's men was a surrender. As soon as one of our men went forward to take them prisoner, he was shot and killed. The result was a serious group of fellow soldiers who vowed never to take a prisoner from that group. The firefight that ensued was over in a few minutes, as it was getting dark and our soldiers withdrew to the village to prepare for the morning attack.

A counterattack was planned for January 4, with e/274 and f/274 in position for the attack. Colonel Cheves told the company commanders to get into town any way they could. Lieutenant Walter Cox captured two houses on the edge of town and from the windows, they looked out on a ghastly sight of gutted and burning buildings. They proceeded to shoot back and forth all day but they could not proceed any further because of the germans firing from inside of the houses in addition to the weather and snow. The attack stopped as neither side wanted to fight at night. The next attack was on the morning of January 5, with Captain Davenport's f/274 in the lead, Lieutenant Cox's Third Platoon of E Company and Lieutenant Meshier's First Platoon following F Company. Captain Dave Davenport and his radio operator and four other soldiers of F Company were hit. Davenport, hit in the arm, refused to quit and kept on going with his men, as was his radioman. Dave was hit twice more and when finally he was hit in the face, he decided to go back for aid. Lieutenant Mahon took over the company and started forward. He was hit in the chest by a sniper and died instantly. The battle raged and it was a furious and bloody fight at close range. Each house held a german and with grenades and rifles, the 70th Division companies advanced. Little by little, the Germans were driven back, but it was obvious now that the enemy was in much greater strength than had been told. F Company was told to hold and now Lieutenant Cox's platoon, along with the others, passed through the front line and encountered heavy fire. Walter came upon a dead German holding a Luger pistol. He wanted to get that pistol but had been trained to ignore the obvious because it might be booby trapped to trip a grenade and kill you, so he moved on and left the pistol on the body. The attack was to shoot any german soldier you could, drop grenades in windows and clear out houses as you progressed through the town. It was slow and as a result of casualties, much time was spent taking care of them and calling for medics. These German SS troops were seasoned soldiers and knew exactly what to do when on the other hand the Americans troops were green with no combat experience.

The very next day, it was an all-day shooting spree between the Germans and our troops. About dark again, with Walter's platoon pinned down in a ditch, another strange thing happened. Walter looked back and standing up on the road behind him was General Thomas Herren, the task force commander. His order to Walter was to get get up and take that town. Walter immediately got up and told his men, "Let's go!" Walter yelled at the general to get down before he got shot and then took off with his platoon toward the first houses in the town. They took two houses and then stopped. During the night, there were fires burning in the town and they could see the Germans going back and forth across the fire. An American jeep came down the road beside one of the houses and the Germans opened fire on it. The men in the jeep jumped out and fled. One of the men came to the house where Walter was staying. After hearing the men speak in English, the men brought him to Walter. He had a grenade in his hand and told Walter he had pulled the pin and it was ready to go off when he released it. Walter obtained some tape and wrapped it around the grenade and tossed it out the window so it would not go off accidentally. One of the men stayed in a ditch, playing dead until morning and almost froze to death but survived. Later on, it was determined that the man was Orville Ellis, who later became president of the Seventieth Division Association. Orville was an executive from St. Louis, Missouri. He directed the association for three years, making it the great association it is today.

The next morning, the soldiers from F Company came by the house on the attack and pushed into town. There were a lot of casualties on both sides. Finally, Walter's company was ordered to progress and move so they fought their way past dead bodies, both German and American losing only a very few of the men under Walter. The fight continue to the Catholic church in the middle of Wingen. Walter sent Sergeant Dyess and Private Dubose up to the door to let the prisoners out. When the door was opened, 300 men came streaming out and the men in Walter's platoon ushered them back through the lines to the rear and out of town. Private First Class Dubose met one of his friends who were in the church for the three days without anything to eat and very little water. It was the first time they had seen each other since basic training. Most of the captives were Forty-fifth Division men, but a few were with the Seventieth having been captured later.

Church at Wingon (prisoners)

The fighting became sporactic and It became apparent that the Germans were either escaping from the village, or were dead or giving up.

After the church was liberated, the Cox platoon went through each house, cleaning out the Germans. This consisted of sending two men in the house to search it for Germans. It was a small village but lots of houses for the two thousand people who lived there but who had left the village when the fighting started. The weather was clear and crisp, but fighting in the severest cold, icy streets was slow and it had to be done so that no soldier could remain in hiding in the village. After a full day with the entire company committed to searching, it was finally declared clear of German soldiers.

To regress back to the heavy fighting when the Company was first committed to the battle, Lieutenant Wayne Meshier, who was the second lieutenant in charge of the First Platoon E Company, jumped out of a window onto the street and was immediately shot in the head. He was dead in a few minutes. This was the first person Walter had seen get shot and killed. He and Meshier were very close as it was Meshier, whom he had ridden to camp in the Cord auto and had been with since the training began, was actually shot and killed in this first combat of his division. Some others in other places had been shot and killed but not in the presence of Walter and were not as close personally as these two.

That night, while Walter and his sergeants were in one of the houses, waiting for dawn, the aggressive tactics would start again and the sound of Germans yelling and making noises of all kinds came out of the woods. A cow was seen coming up the street outside the house. Walter had a feeling that there were Germans on the other side of the cow and ordered his men to kill the cow. It seems that there were three of the enemy hiding on the opposite side of the cow and they also were shot. The counterattack at night had failed and shooting stopped as did the yelling. All night long there was noises from the woods and actions which made the men believe that a german charge was coming None came the balance of the night and at day break, the order was to take the town. It was strange as the platoon moved out to attack. There was no movement from the enemy and no noises. It seems so unusual that the men kept down while moving to the adjoining houses in an effort to route the germans. After many hours of checking all the houses, it was concluded that the SS troopers had withdrawn toward the Rhine river. Thereafter in a book written by the officers of the SS troopers, the withdrawal was confirmed that all those who were alive and could walk were ordered to leave and work their way back to Germany.

The Battle is Won

PRESIDENTIAL CITATION FOR ACTION IN WINGEN

HEADQUARTERS 70th INF DIVISION, APO 461,

U S ARMY   28 July 1945

TO: Commanding Officers, All Units.

    For compliance with 1st indorsement.

        BY COMMAND OF MAJOR GENERAL BARNETT:
            B. V. MERRICK
            Lt. Col. AGD
            Adjutant General

HEADQUARTERS 70th INFANTRY DIVISION

APO 461, US ARMY

GENERAL ORDERS   24 April 1945
NUMBER..... 32

BATTLE HONORS - CITATION OF UNIT

    THE 2D BATTALION, 274th INFANTRY REGIMENT, is cited for outstanding performance in combat during the period 5 to 7 January 1945, at Wingen, France.

    At 1400, 5 January, the 2d Battalion, 274th Inf. received instructions to prepare and occupy a defensive position overlooking the village of Wingen, France. At 2100 on 5 January, this battalion received orders to recapture Wingen which had fallen into German hands on 4 January and which since then had withstood the continuous and costly attacks of an adjacent infantry regiment. Reconnaissance was limited to the intensive study of maps; the nature of the terrain made supplies available only by hand carry down a treacherous ice-covered cliff; the anti-tank guns of the battalion had to be lowered at night by a series of winches over a hazardous mountain trail to accomplish their fire mission; the officers and men of this battalion had been without rest for over sixty hours; the German forces held dominating terrain overlooking the village of Wingen on the battalion's exposed left flank; the only method of receiving any artillery support was by requesting it through the SCR 300 radio of an adjacent battalion.

In spite of these problems, the attack was launched at dawn on 6 January across exposed terrain against numerically superior and fanatically resisting enemy forces in the form of two battalions of the elite German 12th SS Mountain Regiment. The attack continued throughout the day against intensive enemy fire causing a heavy casualty toll in the ranks of the battalion. The gallant esprit de corps of the 2d Battalion was such, however, that by late afternoon over half the village of Wingen was in American hands.

At dusk, the German defenders counterattacked ferociously and succeeded in splitting and isolating the units of the 2d Battalion. With unhesitating disregard of personal safety, the officers and men of this battalion tenaciously hung on to their positions and inflicted such heavy losses on the enemy that the German positions became untenable and an enemy withdrawal was begun during the night. Reorganizing at dawn on 7 January, the battalion attacked again destroying the remnants of the enemy forces. Thus, in two days, the 2d Battalion 274th Infantry, operating under almost insurmountable supply, communication and evacuation problems, in bitter cold, without food or rest, and with the loss of 130 casualties, destroyed two German SS Battalions, liberated over 250 Americans held prisoner by the German forces, recaptured 32 American vehicles, three anti-tank guns, and hundreds of small arms.

The determined fortitude, courage and fighting spirit displayed by members of the 2d Battalion, 274th Infantry, is exemplary of the finest traditions of the American Army and will be inscribed in the annals of the American Infantry.

By Command of Major General BARNETT:
LEO A. BESSETTE
Colonel, GSC
Chief of Staff

OFFICIAL:
B. V. MERRICK
Lt. Col. AGD
Adj. General

The next day, the battalion cleared the entire town and captured the remaining SS troopers. As Walter inspected all the houses, he found one house at the end of the street, where the fighting has been so intense the day before, when Meshier had been killed. In the house, there was a rocking chair at the window with about 200 spent shells on the floor, indicating that the sniper had been the one who had killed Meshier and wounded Captain Davenport, the company commander of Company C and killed Lieutenant Mahon. Incidentally, Captain Dave Davenport was a West Point graduate and was shot three times before he was ordered to return to the medics for treatment. He returned to the battalion in about two months.

The smell of death was all over the village and bodies were everywhere in grotesque shapes because they froze when killed. Soon the truck came and picked up the bodies and stacked them in the truck like firewood. The entire truck was filled with bodies. It is a sight that follows a battle and something that no one wants to see. Losses in the Second Battalion 274 Infantry Regiment of the Seventieth Infantry Division were twenty-five killed and eighty-four wounded. The men of the Seventieth Division were courageous and heroes to a degree that bordered on self-sacrifice. One soldier of E Company simply remembered, "We were green as hell and were up against the toughest soldiers we could ever imagine." Afterward, the German soldiers wrote about their battle with the green troops of the 2nd Battalion. Their book told that the americans were so brave and foolish that they were tough to beat.

During this entire five days, although exposed to enemy fire and artillery, Walter was spared any wounds (angel at work). One of the reasons given by him is the fact that he prayed a lot during the day and night and the fact that he wore a uniform just like his men and carried an M-1 rifle instead of the officer carbine.

Therefore, he was not seen by the enemy as an officer but just as one of the men. Walter told his men that they knew he was there commanding officer and that he did not need any bars or special uniform for them to know who he was. This probably was the most significant decision in keeping him free from being killed or wounded.

The battalion and Walter's Company E were ordered to evacuate to another town for a little rest. After one night's sleep in a small village, Walter and his platoon were ordered into the Vosges Mountains as a defense tactic to keep more infiltration by the enemy. The snow was two or three feet deep and the temperature was below freezing all the time. Foxholes were prepared and trees felled to provide a roof and defense against the cold and the mortar fire. Water had to be carried from a creek nearby and halizone tablets put in the canteens made it somewhat safe. Eating was by K rations, which is a crackerjack box containing a small can of eggs for breakfast, cheese for lunch and meat for dinner. Crackers, instant coffee, three pieces of candy, three cigarettes and the box, which was oiled paper, provided enough heat when burned to heat a canteen to boil coffee. This was all the food that the tough Company soldiers had to eat for the next 6 weeks.

This went on during the month of January and one time, a member of a squad shot a wild pig and the soldiers decided to cook it. The smoke drew mortar fire and of course, the fire went out and no pig meat was eaten much to everyone's dismay. It was a fight to stay alive and one of the great losses of the cold weather was from frozen feet. The direction from the division was to change socks every day and each buddy in the foxholes should massage the feet of his partner and put on dry socks on those cold feet. The wet socks taken from your feet were put inside your shirt next to your undershirt and by the next day, they would be warm and dry and smelly but nice to cold feet. Walter insisted that this procedure be followed and instructed each squad leader to oversee the changing of socks. As a result, none of his platoon ever had to be evacuated because of trench foot (frozen feet).

During this defensive position the men were very well posted so that any movement by the Germans could be seen. As a result of the position, all the Germans did was shoot some artillery into their position and there wereno casualties during the entire time Walter's platoon occupied that mountain.

One night, Second Lieutenant Cox was ordered to go to the Battalion Headquarters. He proceeded down off the mountain and was met by a jeep that carried him to the Battalion Command Post. It was very dark and everything was blackout, so when you entered the door of the house that served as headquarters, through a blanket to black out the light, it was closed behind you and then you entered the lighted room. Immediately upon entering the room, he saw before him the worst-looking soldier he had ever seen. He had a beard, dirty jacket, dirty sweater and dirty greasy pants and looked as if he had been out in a foxhole for thirty days, which obviously he had. It turned out he was looking in a mirror at himself. The colonel laughed at him and said that was what all of them looked like.

A duty was assigned to him and his platoon to go to another location and take over the company position of the first battalion (C Company). The company had lost so many men that there were only thirty men left out of a total of 200. Cox and his forty men were to relieve the thirty men and the process began. His men were brought down to the town and given explicit orders and told this was a very dangerous mission on a steep hillside, with the Germans occupying the high ground above them. The changeover took place quietly and the Germans were not alerted. Foxholes were already dug, so his men just occupied the ones already dug. During the balance of the night, he and his sergeants cleaned and oiled every gun in the platoon. All this was accomplished in complete darkness. All guns were disassembled and put back together in the dark. The manner of cleaning was to spread a blanket on the ground and disassemble the guns, lay out the parts in sequence and clean and reassemble. The training had been explicit and really came in a specific time where it was needed. The morning brought gunfire from above and was returned by Cox's men. After the first assault, there was no attack during the day, which was a relief to Walter. That night, more orders were received. According to the order, the seventh army had advanced, but the Seventieth Division had penetrated further than the rest of the army. It appeared that the Regimental commander, Shooting Sam Conley was a west pointer and wanted to be a General, so he ordered the regiment to attack more than other regiments.

The entire regiment had advanced too far in front of the entire Seventh Army front and were in danger of being cut off from the rear, so a withdrawal was ordered by the Seventieth Division commander, General Thomas Herren (picture) Cox and his platoon were ordered to be the covering rifle platoon, together with Major Paul Durbin, the senior officer and assistant battalion commander in charge of the covering force. The fighting group led by Cox's platoon included a heavy machine gun squad, a mortar squad and several bazooka men. The entire division left their positions about midnight and walked ten miles to the rear, leaving Cox and Durbin with their men at a crossroad where the Germans would probably travel if they found out there was a withdrawal. Actually it was a suicide mission because all the men could do was delay the Germans until they were killed or wounded.

Major Durbin was ordered to stay and cover until daybreak. About 3:00 a.m., Major Durbin asked Cox if he could see the sun coming up. Since it was only February 1, the nights were long and, of course, there was no sun, but Cox's reply was "Yes, sir, I see the sun." The trucks and the men that were left for the covering force withdrawal were soon on the move to the rear. By 4:00 a.m., all the troops were in place ten miles to the rear; and by God's help, the withdrawal had not been discovered—angel at work. As a side tale, several men were asleep when the withdrawal was ordered and did not get out of their foxholes and were left behind and captured the next day. Some of those men joined the Seventieth Division Association later and told the tale of waking up with the Germans looking down into their foxholes.

As a side issue, the trailblazer magazine of the Seventieth Division Association carried a story about the Durbins. They celebrated their Seventieth wedding anniversary in Hawaii, the final resting place after all the military he had been in. He is ninety-two and she is ninety-one. On April 8, 2012, Paul died in Hawaii.

During the days that followed, nothing transpired and the division was readied for the attack on the Seigfried line at Saarbrucken, across the Saar River. By late February, the jump-off was preceded by patrols going out to try to determine where the enemy line started. One night, Sergeant Murphy was sent out on a patrol to check the front of E Company and another company sent out a patrol to do the same but in a different sector. Getting lost in the dark was easy and the patrols ran into each other. Murphy was shot and killed by one of the other company men. Cox was in the Company Headquarters when one of his men carried Murphy on his back into the HQ. What a waste!

Cox had been promoted to company executive officer during this month and was promoted to first lieutenant. The day of the attack, Walter told the company kitchen personnel to go find eggs, ham, biscuits and other items for a great breakfast, which may be the last one for some of the men. They started feeding before daybreak and each man had his eggs exactly the way he wanted them. They also had bacon, biscuits, jelly, juice and coffee.

At 7:00 a.m., the entire division pushed off in attack. It was about two or three miles before coming in contact with the Germans. When that happened, many of the companies came up against resistance from the tanks, machine guns, mortar and other weapons. A lot of men were wounded and killed, but the division kept moving until night when everything stopped. The woods were thick and there were firebreaks in them, which was a trap for the men to go from one forest to cross over 100 yards with no trees to hide behind. Once the men entered the forests ahead, the Germans ordered the tanks to shoot into the trees and the bursts of steel hit the trees and down onto the men, wounding even more. With much maneuvering and getting into a place where the bazooka teams could fire on the tanks, the tanks withdrew and the company moved forward. There were fingers of hills with deep ravines in between and each Company moved along the top of the ridges.

E Company occupied the left ridge and fought down the ridge until a bunker was captured, which was then occupied by Captain Sisson, Company Commander of E Company and Walter, who was executive officer of the company and other HQ personnel. The very next morning, a squad of Germans came up a ravine on the left and cut off the entire company. Captain Sisson ordered Cox to go down the opposite ravine in order to contact F Company, whose company commander was Charles Eblen (Hook was his nickname when he played football for the University of Kentucky) and which occupied the other ridge and to organize a squad of men to counterattack the Germans who held the ground above E Company. All the way down the hill to the bottom and then back up the ridge by himself, praying all the time and feeling sure he would be shot by either the Germans or F Company men, Cox was careful and when he neared the ridge, he yelled to the men telling them who he was and that he needed to come to them. His prayers were answered and soon he had the squad ready to counterattack (angel on shoulder). Captain Eblen, who was Company Commander, gave him the best men he had and soon Walter and the soldiers with 30-caliber light machine guns and M-1 rifles were blazing the woods as they attacked down the ridge. The machine gun was held by a sergeant who held it at his hip and another soldier held the bullets as they were fed into the machine gun. Walter walked along with the machine gunner and was impressed by the efficiency of the soldiers of F company. Soon they came upon the dead Germans who had made the counterattack. They were either dead or wounded and the battle was finished. It made an impression on all the soldiers and Walter to see the germans lying in foxholes dead or wounded. The men were young and innocent even though they were ordered to kill the Americans and had made every effort to do so. Now they were finished and their war was over. At one occasion while beginning the attack on the top of the hill overlooking the village of Stirling Wendell, Walter and a forward observer in a fox hole dug by some of the troops. They observed the light plane calling for artillery diving and climbing between shells being dropped by both americans and germans. The town was on fire and hundreds of shells were falling. It was as if a movie was being filmed and shown on the screen. Nothing like the real thing, however.!!!!!!!!!!!!!!

The next day, the attack to the Saar river by E Company continued and down the hill they went. Walter was scouting in front and all at once, a crack of a bullet went over his head. Walter fell as if hit so the Germans would think and not shoot again. Lucky again. (Angel) They continued down the hill until they were in a flat level area just short of the Metz Highway, which connected Saarbrucken and the towns in France, namely Stirling Wendell and Forbach. B Company was on the right and Cox and Lieutenant George Dudley were both executive officers in charge. They decided to form a perimeter defense for the night with both companies and proceeded to form a circle (1500 yards or more), with the two of them in a foxhole in the middle. Everyone dug in and Cox and Dudley dug a foxhole in fifteen minutes. The soil was loamy and once you broke through the snow and ice, it was fairly easy. Each foxhole was occupied by two men and the order was one man sleeping and one awake.

During the night, Cox was awakened by the soldiers of the wire section bringing a phone to the foxhole. (The communication section of the company were to keep contact with the companies by stringing wire to the forward units.) Both Cox and Dudley were asleep and it appeared that all the men in both companies were also asleep. Quickly, all were awakened and warned not to go back to sleep. As soon as daybreak came, a sergeant came to Cox and told him that a squad of Germans were marching up the Metz Highway, completely unaware that the two companies were occupying the land. The sergeant was told to shoot and that he and his men did. The firefight continued until both companies E and B crossed the highway and went into the town of Stirling Wendell. They fought and occupied as much of town as was possible, shooting and throwing grenades and capturing German soldiers. The following days were spent in pushing through the town and then things stopped for a few days. Cox was called back to battalion and told he was to be the new company commander of Company E. He was told he was to be provided new second lieutenants or he could make his sergeants commissioned officers with a battlefield promotion. Cox chose the latter and promoted four sergeants to the rank of second lieutenants.

The fighting went on through the town, pushing the Germans out of the towns bordering the Saar River. AmericanTanks would come up into the towns to help protect the infantry. While in a position beside a house, Walter saw a mortar squad of Germans shoot off a screaming meemie (sort of mortar that shot large shells that were so slow you could hear them coming) up in the hills just short of the Saar River. He jumped up on a tank to show the tankers the emplacement of the german mortar squad and about that time, one went off. The Germans had seen Cox and shot one toward the tank. Walter jumped off the tank and spread out on the cobblestone street as flat as possible. The shell hit very close (with an umbrella effect) and luckily (angel) the shrapnel went over the top of Walter and never hit him. There was a little sliver of metal in his thigh but so small it was not reported.

The 2nd Battalion Co E continued to map up pockets of resistance in the city. The enemy was engaged in bitter house to house fighting in the town of Stirling-Wendel. During the day the enemy fired heavy mortar and artillery concentrations. Co E now being commanded by Walter came upon several hundred allied prisoners of war who made their way into the city after leaving the Prisoner of War hospital, north of the city. An enemy machine gun opened fire on these men, wounding serveral, as they walked down the Metz Highway. Walter's Company returned the fire and later captured the hospital. A total 1000 prisoners of war mostly Russian but including polish, French, Czechs and Yugoslavs were liberated.

The offensive operation of 17 February 1945 until March 7, the 70th Division had liberated eighteen towns and taken 2034 prisoners including 14 officers. The Division had repulsed 29 counterattacks.

Lt General Patch, commanding general 7th Army, along with 70th Division commander, General Barnett toured the 70th Division sector. On the19 of March, the 7oth infantry divison was ordered to forcea crossing of the Saar River, sieze the objectives, establish a bridgehead and to reduce Saarbrucken.

After weeks of battling back and forth, the Seventh Army ordered the division to cross the Saar River at Saarbrucken, but the Colonels of the first, second and third battalions refused to cross the river, saying it would be pure suicide. Major Paul

Durbin was appointed as commander of the Third Battalion and was ordered to cross the Saar River. He went back to the HQ and talked to colonel SHOOTIN SAM CONLEY who was in charge of the 274 Regiment for three days. Finally, the regiment did cross into Saarbrucken. Cox's Company E was one of the first to cross the river on pontoon boats that had been pushed across the river at night by the American engineers. After twenty-four hours of continuous shelling and mortar, apparently the Germans decided to withdraw from the bunkers and the entire city of Saarbrucken. As a result, there were no casualties. Thank God! (Angel). The orders came down from battalion officers for E Company to make contact with the German soldiers and to get on anything mechanical and get rolling if possible. The men found trucks, bicycles, motorcycles, horses and anything to make them move fast. Walter took over a small motor scooter and used it to keep the company moving and together. The end of the day found E Company at Dudweiler, Germany, about sixteen miles deep into Germany . . .

The Division assumed responsibility for Third Army (Pattons army) lines of communication and rear areas, Rhine River-Boppard, Oberndorff and Oppenheim. By late April, the division was responsible for patrolling and guarding several hundred installations such as railroad beidges, supply depots, hospitals, airports, government building, electric plants, dams and public utilities, fod and warehouse, roadblocks, roads and supply routes covering several thousands of miles.

The houses were intact, with phones, electricity and radios working. The men took over for the night. Cox posted guards and went to sleep in a feather bed. The next morning, very early, a sergeant came excitedly into the bedroom and announced that a company of German soldiers were waiting on the road outside, their firearms stacked and ready to surrender. Cox immediately went to the street and took the surrender from the officer in charge, turning the Germans over to some of his men to take back to an area for prisoners.

After that narrow escape, which could have been fatal for all his company, the next towns taken were very carefully searched before sleeping. In each small village, the town mayor would be contacted and ordered to tell all occupants to bring all weapons to the town hall and turn them over to his company. This was done and then on to other towns. Walter would let his men pick pistols and cameras for themselves when the German population turned them in to the town hall. A few soldiers would come out and surrender, but most ran. After many days of this type of operation, the company reached Frankfurt, Germany, the division was ordered to stop and to complete searching procedures and to secure the city. General Patton and the Third Division had cut off the Seventieth Infantry Division and the Seventieth soldiers were to go no further. (Thanks to his angel.) Walter always thought Patton to be his hero after that.

The real war was over for his men. Cleanup and capture of German soldiers left behind was an easy duty and as a result, no one was killed after that.

Walter and Private First Class Chavez, the driver of his jeep, were driving around the city and next to the river, doing investigative duty when all at once, the driver looked down on the ground and could see the round marks on the ground that indicated there were mines. The jeep had been driven in between the mines and missed hitting one of them. Cox told Chavez to back up on the same tracks they made getting up to river. They made it back without the mines being hit (whew) and reported them to the engineers, who disabled the mine field. During this occupation of Frankfurt, the Rhine River was watched carefully to make sure no Germans were floating down the river to attack from the rear. There were bodies taken from the river every day, both American and German, which obviously had been engaged in crossing the river upstream and were just now floating down the stream.

The men raided the wine cellars and had a great time for a while. They found champagne, wine, liqueurs, cognac and all kinds of liquor.

End of World War II in Germany May 8, 1945. Just after the death of President Franklin Roosevelt. Vice President, Harry Truman assumed the Presidency at that time and was President when the War ended.

The war was over for them and within thirty days, by May 8, 1945, the war was declared finished. A peace treaty was signed by General Eisenhower. Some semblance of normalcy reigned. A celebration was planned and the entire division marched down the Main Street in Frankfurt, Germany, on May Day. There were

Walter Leading his Company Frankfurt Germany

other activities on the River Rhine and food to eat. Walter marched in front of his company. Shortly thereafter, Cox received orders to take his company to the small area on the Rhine River close by and occupy a beautiful villa (see pic of villa) overlooking the Rhine River. It was equipped with a swimming pool, a dining room large enough for his company to eat in and a bowling alley overlooking the river in the Wine Country. There they established a routine and started training for the landing in Japan. It was relatively safe, as the Germans were generally glad to have a world without war and were very cooperative and docile. Only when Cox filled the swimming pool with water were they mad because he had drained the entire drinking water reservoir of the small village. The men of E Company had a wonderful mess hall in the great room of the villa. There was plenty of good food and wine to drink. The villa had a large dining room so that the entire company could eat inside the villa. There was a bar established and the wine flowed freely.

One night, when Walter and his officers were on the Rhine River, at the officers' club, a soldier with a rifle took over the Company Command Post and told anyone who came in that he would shoot them. When Walter returned, the sergeant who was officer of the day told Walter about the incident. Walter immediately went to the C.P. and told the soldier he was coming in and to put his rifle down and surrender. It apparently worked because as Walter entered the room, the soldier put his rifle down. The soldier had drunk too much wine and was out of control. Walter as company commander gave the soldier company punishment rather than courts-martial. He made him dig a hole six feet deep by six feet square and then fill it up again. All the others watched this being done and from then on, there was no infraction of rules.

Walter 3rd from left Company E Commander

The division had orders to train for landings in Japan, so every day the company trained to go across the Rhine River and land on the other side as if it were to take place somewhere in Japan. This was an unhappy thought and soon was changed.

This took place on the latter days of June 1945 and in July, a transformation took place. The men of the Seventieth Infantry Division transferred to the Third Division and the men of the Third Division were sent home, along with those in the Seventieth Division who were lucky enough to be needed for the trip home. The Seventieth became the cadre (soldiers) for the Third Division and Cox was sent along with some of his men to Phillipsthal, Germany, on the Russian Border as Executive Company Commander of "A" Company, The Russians and Americans had established a line between East and West Germany and Cox's company guarded the border. The East Germans were escaping to West Germany as fast as they could. The Russians had searchlights all along the border, which rotated from left to right at regular intervals. At night, when there was no moon and the searchlights of the Russians were turning, the children, men and women would run as fast as possible to cross over to the American West sector. The mission of A Company First Battalion, Seventh Infantry Regiment was to collect the defectors and take them to HQ the next morning for briefing and medical help. About 100 each night would come across into the company area and would be kept in a barn until morning. This went on from June 1945 until September 1945, with the continuous stream of German civilians coming from the east to escape the wrath of the Russian Army. The women had been raped; and the men, beaten, which was the way the Russians soldiers treated them all. Most of the women had a venereal disease or other infirmities.

While Walter was executive officer of the company, he received a bulletin from the division that VD (venereal disease) was out of hand. The directive was to establish a VD station in each company for the men. It was to be manned twenty-four hours a day. In some companies, the percentage was as high as 70 percent of the men contracting VD. Walter established a session for every man in the company to attend which would tell them about the terrible aftereffects of VD. He related the fact that they may never get well from it and may carry it home to their loved ones. That it could cause all kinds of problems that could last forever, such as blindness, brain damage, deformity, etc. From that time on, Walter's company had the best record of all the division from not contracting VD. It was a fact that most of the Germans girls had contracted VD.

While the men of the Russian Army were very badly treated, not having good food or clothes, they were given the same occupation money that the American Army were given; therefore, the Russians would buy anything the American soldier would sell them. It included watches, food, clothes, weapons and other items. Some Russians invited Walter and his officers to have dinner with them at their house in the Russian territory. They had a great meal and the Russians drank vodka as if it were water. Walter watched with great interest but stayed away from the vodka. Communication was a problem, but Walter had an interpreter with him so he could understand what they were saying. It seems that the Russians took everything from all the

German homes, including kitchen and bathroom fixtures and shipped them by rail back to Russia.

After a month or so, Cox was transferred to the Battalion Headquarters to take over as S1 Adjutant of the First Battalion, Seventh Infantry Regiment, Third Division. In that capacity, he was battalion headquarters company commander as well as head of all the battalion Company, serving only under the battalion commander. He was billeted in a modern house built by the Nazis in the 1930s for the well-to-do Germans (see pic of house). In this house was the officers' mess, which fed about ten officers. The motor pool officer and a medical officer also occupied rooms in the house. The meals were superb and Cox had sent for and obtained the best chef in the town. The chef had been a chef in a hotel before the war. With trading cigarettes, coffee and other hard to get items, the staff of the kitchen was able to procure the best meat, chicken, vegetables, eggs, ice cream and fruit. A violinist played for dinner each evening for the officers and of course, there was wine and cognac for all to enjoy. The officers of the first battalion 7th infantry, 3rd Division were a great group of officers and were enjoying the occupation of Germany.

In August, Walter received a directive that one officer could go to the French Riviera to a town called Cannes. Walter asked the battalion commander for permission to take this trip and was given that authority. This town was occupied only by officers. The transportation was by a C47, a cargo plane that could only fly low and the only window was small holes in the sides of the plane. The plane was not pressurized and the seats were metal along the sides of the plane. It flew close to the Alps, with snow on top, which was a sight to see. After 2 days at Cannes, the most wonderful thing happened. President Harry Truman ordered the atomic bomb to be dropped in Japan. After one more day and one more bomb being dropped, the Japanese finally surrendered. Celebration after celebration took place.

Walter in Cockpit

Cannes France

Villa in Germany on Rhine River

While at Cannes, Walter ran into some of the officers of Company G of the University of Kentucky, who had been sent to other divisions during the fighting in Germany. They as was Walter, simply astounded and excited about the end of the war in Japan. During the time they spent in celebrating they exchanged stories about their combat experiences.

Back in Hersfield, life went on and the men all carried side arms, a pistol and belt with ammunition at all times but never used. The motor pool officer, Lieutenant Ableson, procured a 1933 German automobile (opal capitan)They painted it olive drab with numbers that identified it as an American vehicle and all the officers at various times enjoyed motoring around the various towns on the weekends. Life was great as it should be for the victors for the months of October through December 1945. During January 1946, Walter contacted strep throat, ran a fever and was pretty sick. The medical doctor who lived in the same house as Walter prescribed penicillin, which had just been introduced into the medical field. During the war, nothing like that wonderful drug existed until after the war was over. It was so new that it was administered every three hours by needle. The doctor would give Walter the shots all day and then wake him up during the night and shoot him a couple of times. Walter was sick for about two weeks and that is the only time during War II that he had any reason to receive medical attention. It did seem that after the war was over, Walter's gums bled after brushing and the doctor said that all he needed was fresh salads and vitamin C, so after two months and eating properly, the bleeding abated. Hersfeld was about 60 kilometers from Frankfurt so once a week, Walter would take a few officers and go to Sheaff headquarters in Frankfurt where the fabulous buffet of that headquarters was located. Every type of food, salads, vegetables, desserts, ice cream and liquors were served daily. This was Esinhowers head quarters and was the most elaborate that could be imagined. In addition there was a military store called a PX that was fully equipped with anything type of military clothes that one could imagine. Walter and others bought new clothes and lots of trinkets.

Walter & Opal Capitan

Headquarters Hersfeld Germany

Another directive was received from HQ and Cox volunteered for duty for a week in Paris, which consisted of attending the University of Paris for education to be used in the occupation of Germany. When he arrived there by command vehicle, he was assigned a hotel and told to go to the university every day for four hours' education. During the time at the university, the instructors talked about the occupation of Germany and the education of the men under his command. When the lectures were over, he was free to go anywhere. He and the two other officers visited the Lido Club, where the floor shows were spectacular, with girls without tops. The shows there and at

Pigalle were the main attractions for the soldiers as you can imagine. Then on to the Folies Bergère, where chorus lines of beautiful French girls danced topless. He also saw the other sites, such as the Cathedral of Notre Dame, Eiffel Tower, Champs de lessin and other tourist attractions.

Walter in Paris France

One of the instructors invited Walter to attend a dinner with his family and friends. The home was lavish and the dinner was unlike anything Walter had ever experienced. There was beautiful china, crystal and all the nicest dinnerware that could be found. They served one course at a time and between courses, there would be a small bowl of one dip of sherbet to clean your palate or so they said. Walter ate everything and from 8:00 p.m. until 11:00 p.m., the dinner continued. What an interesting affair and Walter never forgot that night.

Later on, during the winter of 1946, he also volunteered to attend a week at the University of Heidelberg for additional education. The town of Heidelberg is an educational arena and was intentionally off limits during the bombing by England and America. It dates back to the early AD 800 and has very unusual architecture. Walter learned all about what was expected of the occupation troops while living in Germany. The education received at Heidelberg was about occupation and how to treat the Germans.

Walter in Switzerland

Around Christmas of 1945, Cox obtained seven days leave to visit Switzerland. The trip was by train to the border of Germany and Switzerland. The entrance to Switzerland was like going to a fairyland. The stores were filled with everything, the food was just like America and the electric trains took him on a trip each day to a different city and hotel.

During the time there, he purchased as many inexpensive $1 watches as he could carry back in his bloused trousers. Boots were worn with trousers tucked in the boots. He also bought Omega watches for his brother, Glen, his dad and mother and Mary Lee. When he got back to his town, he went to the Russian border and sold the dollar watches for $100 each. It seems that the Russians had the same paper money that was issued to the Americans. He could not send the money back to the States, as he could send only the amount he was paid. Eachsoldier had a book where all income and money sent home was recorded. As a result, Walter had a lot of money to spend in Germany. He had clothes made for his return to law school, had hand-painted pictures of he and Mary Lee, done from photos; and bought a few articles as mementoes. In March 1946, Walter received a promotion to captain, which was too long in coming but was a welcome sight to see the two silver bars instead of the one silver bar of a first lieutenant. The pay was pitiful for a first lieutenant which was about $300 per month, so a raise of $60 per month was a large increase of 20%.

The event of the time which was winter of 1945-46 was the death of General Patton. It was reported in the army newspaper (stars and stripes) that there had been an auto accident in which Patton was riding. It stated that the Cadillac in which he was riding down the autobahn highway was hit by an army truck that pulled in front of the vehicle occupied by Patton. The General was thrown from the back seat up against the front seat and suffered a broken neck. A specialist medical surgeon was sent for (from Louisville, Ky) and arrived in a couple of days. Obviously the operation was unsuccessful because his death came in 5 days. At the time, Patton had been relieved of his command because he was talking about attacking Russia and or conquering the entire western Europe. There were rumors that he had been intentionally killed to avoid the publicity he was getting when he took his stand on the idea of an invasion. It was obvious that General Eisenhouer was upset about his ideas. Patton was a great officer and keep on fighting was all he wanted to do.

During the spring, Walter and his fellow officers, including the other officers of the battalion, visited a salt mine near Hersfield, Germany, where the headquarters was located. The elevator took them down one mile into the earth to shafts extending into all directions. Small vehicles took them through the shafts to the storage area of the Berlin Opera costumes. There were, it seemed, miles of costumes of all kinds and shapes. It was reported that they were stored there to protect them from rot as it was extremely dry having the salt to keep down humidity. Upon reporting this discovery to the colonel who commanded the entire regiment, he suggested that the officers have a costume party and dance. They immediately planned and obtained over one hundred costumes from the salt mine. The party was a blast and the Seventieth band played for the costumed ladies and officers at the officers' club. The women were nurses from a local hospital and they dressed in period costumes with wigs and shoes and all as if it were in the 1700s. The officers had various costumes with leggings, unusual shoes, wigs and sashes. All the costumes were returned to the salt mine after the party. Thereafter, the Regimental Commander, Colonel Heinckes whose father had fought in War I with the Germans) received a reprimand from the division. Cox was called in by the Colonel and was told that he had been instrumental in the

Walter on right Hersfeld Germany

reprimand. Cox said he was sorry, but the entire regimental officers had a good time and deserved it. The Colonel replied, "To hell with them. I had a good time and the Germans be damned" (as they had complained about the use of the Berlin Opera costumes).

274th Infantry officers Club in Germany

In Hersfeld, where the headquarters were located, there was a tennis court. During the season, some of the officers tried to play tennis and enjoy the sunshine (see picture of Walter Tennis Rackets). During the time from October 1945 until Walter had trips to Paris, France, Switzerland and a week in Heidleburg, Germany, each being a week long. On December 20, 1945, he called Mary Lee from

Tennis in Hersfeld

Switzerland and it was the first time to talk since leaving her in Lancaster on November 10, 1944. It took six hours to arrange the phone call from her to Walter. Walter enjoyed the trip to Switzerland more than all the other cities he had visited. The swiss trains were electric and wound their way around miles of mountains and tunnels. If the train was scheduled to leave on 1156 A. M. it would pull out on the exact minute and arrive at the exact minute according to schedule. The food was delicious and the facilities were superb.

In May 1946, Walter received orders to return home and to be dismissed from the service in June. It was a long way home through Camp Lucky Strike in Normandy, France. Finally, after trading some occupation money and some firearms, he was able to obtain some good old American dollars to take home. Walter took six revolvers to the port of embarkation but upon arriving, found that he could take only one pistol home. He sold the five to officers who still had money they could send home and he kept only the German Luger.

On board the Victory Ship, he was named Security Officer and had the run of the ship. He visited every part of the ship, from the captain's quarters to the engine room. He rode the bow of the small ship up and down in the waves as if it were a seesaw and enjoyed the rough ride without getting seasick. He would ride in the bow of the ship and it would go up and down like a roller coaster. The trip took seven days and Walter did not get seasick during the entire rough ride.

Arriving in New York, there was a two-day delay in route to Camp Atterbury, where the final release would take place. Several officers were going to Coney Island to see the sights and Walter went along. While riding the roller coaster, he mused that he might be killed on that damn coaster after having survived the entire war. They then visited a famous restaurant named Leon and Eddies. What a great place to celebrate.

Walter on Right - Leon & Eddies Restaurant

At Camp Atterbury, after Walter was told he could receive his reserve commission for a period of five additional years or could give it up and when he was recalled, he would have to start over as a second lieutenant, he accepted and signed for five more years as a captain.

Walter had been talking to his wife, Mary Lee and she was to meet him in Lexington on his release. Five other officers were going to Louisville, so the six of them piled in a taxi and went sixty miles in a crazy taxi whose driver seemed bent on killing them. They arrived safely, however and Walter caught a bus to Lexington. It was so crowded that he had to stand up the entire way.

Discharge from the Army

In Lexington, Mary Lee and another couple, Butch Little and his girlfriend, were with her and drove them to London, Kentucky. They stayed in London a couple of days and then went on the Lancaster to see Walter's family. After the final day in Lancaster, Kentucky, Walter and Mary Lee departed on an extended honeymoon.

Mary Lee & Walter

They had been apart from November 10, 1944, until June 25, 1946, so it was a wonderful homecoming. It was so great that their first baby, Mary Eugenia was born nine months from the day that Walter came home, June 25 to March 24, 1947. Mary Lee and Walter went on a delayed honeymoon for two weeks to Lexington, Cincinnati, Canada, Niagara Falls, Washington DC and other stops along the way. One stop in Washington was interesting because as they drove to downtown DC, they observed dancing on top of a hotel, so they checked in the hotel, dressed and went on up to the rooftop restaurant. Mary Lee had just purchased a new black and white dress, which was quite attractive and she wanted to show it off. When they arrived at the rooftop restaurant patio where the dancing was taking place, lo and behold, there was another lady dressed in a dress just like Mary Lee's. We all laughed about it and became friends. But Mary Lee never forgot that night and told the story many times.

During the trip, Walter had to wear his uniform, as he was on leave from the military and drawing pay. Walter encountered a new America when men who had obviously been in the Army or Navy made slurring remarks about him being an officer. Why they were mad at officers was beyond his imagination because all his men were extremely happy and never said anything derogatory about officers.

During June 1946 until August 31, he actually received an increase in his pay, as all military were upgraded to a new pay scale. After August, he was finally discharged from active duty with the army and did not wear the uniform any longer.

Back home, the next item was to get ready to reenter law school and to find a place to live. Mary Lee and Walter obtained a real-estate agent in Lexington and went around to find a place to rent, but none could be found. Next, it was a decision to buy a house and Walter Sr. said they could borrow the money on a note that he would cosign. A house was found on Bucoto Court in Lexington for the large sum of $7,500. The contract was made and the loan was 4 percent interest with the interest only being paid every six months. So $150 would be paid every six months out of the total sum of $120 per month being paid to them by the GI Bill for veterans. They rented a room to another couple that were from London for $35 per month, which covered the interest.

While living in the house with their dog, Pepper, there were rats out in the backyard. Walter had a .22 rifle and he would shoot the rats from the back door. They also applied to the Shawnee Town student apartment housing so that when it came up, they could sell the house and move there. Mary Eugenia was born on March 24, 1947 and neither Walter or Mary Lee knew anything about taking care of a baby, so Mary Lee's mom lived with them until June of 1947, when the housing was offered to them and they put the house on the market and sold it for the net sum of $7,500, getting out of it what they paid for it. The housing at the University of Kentucky was $29 per month including all utilities. It consisted of a small bath, kitchen, bedroom and living room and was heated by a kerosene stove located in the middle of the small living room. The kitchen also had a kerosene stove with four burners. By this time, March 24, 1947, Mary Eugenia was born on a windy night at the Good Sam Hospital. Ms. Engle, Mary Lee's mother, was on hand and she and Walter listened to the finals at Madison Square Garden for the UK basketball. At 11:30 p.m., the cats won and Eugenia was born about the same time. She was and is a beautiful girl and looked just like Walter.

The very next day, March 25, Walter woke up to a twelve-inch snow and could not get the car out of a snowdrift, so he had to walk to the hospital and to law school. Eugenia nicknamed Jeannie and Mary Lee stayed in the Good Samaritan for a full week before Dr. Whitehouse would allow them to come home. The doctor's bill was $75 and the Hospital bill was $200—a lot different than today. Upon arriving home, the baby bed had been established and the cocker spaniel named Pepper welcomed Jeannie home. Jeannie slept during the day and stayed up all night with the colic and Walter almost fell asleep in classes several times. After a couple of months, the apartment at Shawnee Town came available and the family moved to Shawnee Town. The house was sold for the same amount that Walter had paid for it. The people who bought the house sanded the floors of the house on Bucoto Court and the floors were eaten up by termites. Walter saw the floor and was extremely glad they had sold the house before finding the termite problem. In the veterans' apartments, the bedrooms were next to each other. The couple in the adjoining apartment had a little girl of the same age as Jeannie and when one was crying, the other joined in, so it continued all night. That summer of 1947, polio was prevalent in Lexington and Mary Lee took Jeannie and went to London and stayed almost all summer to escape the epidemic. Luckily, we were not affected by polio.

One night, Mary Lee heard crying coming from the end apartment in the project. After opening a window and entering the apartment, Walter found the couple's little three-year-old boy tied to his bed. He and Mary Lee untied him and took him to their apartment. When the couple arrived back home, Walter was ready and waiting and warned them that they had done the unthinkable and would not be reported, but they were never to do anything of that kind again.

That fall, Walter attended a football game with some of the law school students and drank too much bourbon. Kentucky won 60 to 7.

Walter got home but was so out of it that he slept outside until morning, when he could finally begin to be normal. That was the last time Walter ever drank too much. Diapers had to be washed and there was a building that had automatic clothes washing machines in it, where the diapers were washed but there were no dryers. Therefore, they had to be hung on a clothes line for drying, which was provided for by the project. The only problem they would freeze solid and would have to be taken in the apartment to thaw out. Because of the humidity in the apartment, both he and Mary Lee had colds and sinus problems all winter.

Law school took up most all of Walter's time, although he did work for the law library, keeping it clean and neat by putting up books at fifty cents per hour. In the summer of 1948, when he was finishing the last semester of law school, polio was taking its toll on kids, so Mary Lee went to London to get away from Lexington to protect Jeannie. All this time, Walter was studying for the bar exam. Four or five students would get together in one of the apartments and go over various study books with questions and answers. This went on for four or five weeks before the exam was scheduled. Finally, the time came and the exam took place in Frankfort, Kentucky, at the House of Representatives. It took three days and was entirely in narrative form. Walter wrote 120 pages of answers in long hand during the taking of the bar exam.

During the three-day exam, there was one prospective lawyer who was a straight A student that came in the last of the exam days drunk. He was taken away and the exam had to be taken again the next time it was given. This same guy finally became a lawyer and one Friday, when Judge Bradley was trying divorce cases, the lawyer who had drunk too much during a bar exam, showed up to try a divorce case and it he was drunk again. When he leaned over to give papers to Judge Bradley, he fell in the judge's lap. Judge Bradley saw Walter standing in the door, watching and asked him to finish trying the case for the drunk. About ten years later, the guy died of liver failure.

After the bar exam was taken, it was about 6 weeks before hearing of the results and by that time, he had moved his family to Lancaster and bought a house. He spent his time cleaning the office of Green Clay Walker, the attorney, former judge and former county attorney who had ask Walter to office with him. The office was on the second floor over a men's store. The twenty steps up were steep and inside, there was a coal stove they used to heat, a fan to cool and a wall telephone. The one large office consisted of two desks for each of them and bookcases that held the old books that had been collected by Lewis Walker, a member of the Eightieth Congress and the brother of Green Clay Walker. There was a quarter inch of dust on everything and Walter cleaned it all and varnished the bookcases. He also ordered desk telephones for each.

New Lawyer

One day, the news came from a classmate that all who had studied together had all passed the bar exam. Plans were in place to go to the Golden Horseshoe restaurant in Lexington to celebrate. The restaurant was the best in the city and Ralph Campbell, the owner, would stand at the entrance from the walk to the door with a heavy woven golden rope and keep the crowd back until room was made inside. He would call you "Doctor" if he did not know your name and everybody loved the guy. The new lawyers celebrated with their wives and, the next day or two, drove to Frankfort to be sworn in as a lawyer. All the students who had passed the bar were sworn in by the judge at the Court of Appeals in the Representatives Chamber.

Back at the office in Lancaster, Walter hung up his shingle made out of black and gold with a sign of Notary Public hanging under the attorney shingle. The following week, after being admitted to the bar, he and all the other new attorneys were called to Frankfort, where they were sworn in by the Kentucky Supreme Court. That was very impressive and Walter always remembers that day as a day that changed his life. Then back at the old office, he waited for a client. Green Clay told him to grab a file and run to the courthouse every morning and afternoon so people would think he was busy. A few men brought him a deed or two to do and that was about all. One man came to him and asked him to represent him in Stanford on the charge of spouging (catching fish with hands). The sheriff who arrested his client was put on the stand to testify. On cross-exam, Walter asked him if his client caught any fish. He answered that he didn't but was trying to. Walter asked the judge for a directed verdict on grounds that the client did not violate any law by being in the water, looking as if he was catching fish. The judge dismissed the case and Walter charged his client $25, making a win out of his first case.

Walter joined the Kiwanis Club of Lancaster and lo and behold, the sixteen Kiwanians voted him as president for the year 1949. It turned out that when the district convention was held in Lexington, Walter was the youngest president in all Kiwanis at twenty-six years of age. In January 1949, Green Clay had a lot of income tax clients and he asked Walter if he would learn to do income tax. He went to school for two days in Lexington and set to work doing income tax. At that time, farmers had to file by January 31 so everyone in the county had to do that chore in the thirty days. People would line up on the stairway and take their turn at his desk to do their tax. That was enough to keep him busy for the entire month and then on into the next few months.

Judge Kendrick Alcorn was the Circuit Judge and when he came to town, all the lawyers were in the court room. The first day of court, Judge Alcorn called Walter up to the bench and told him to take this man back to the witness room and to be ready for trial in thirty minutes. The twenty-one-year-old man was charged with concealing a deadly weapon (*towit*), a knife over six inches long. This charge carried a prison sentence of two years. There was no defense as the guy admitted the charge, so Walter talked to the prosecutor and arranged for a twelve-month sentence to be probated. The man was tickled and promised to pay Walter when he went to work, which he did pay $50 over a period of time.

The November 1948 election was held two months after Walter came eligible to practice law. That was the year that President Truman was reelected after becoming vice president in 1944 and then president after President Roosevelt died just before World War II was over. The morning after the election, Walter was called to the courthouse and told he had been elected Police Judge for Lancaster. His fellow veterans at the American Legion and Veterans of Foreign Wars had written him in as a candidate. The year 1948 was the year Harry Truman was reelected over Tom Dewey. Walter was a registered Democrat and voted for Harry but went to bed thinking Tom Dewey had won the election. When Walter woke up and listened to the radio, Harry had won by a small margin.

The position of City Judge was paid only $50 per month, but he took it and had fun holding court each morning at 8:00 a.m. Drunks, drivers exceeding the limit, fights, wife beaters and other abusers of the law were brought before him for guilty or not guilty pleas. Walter instituted a new procedure for paying fines. When an employer wanted to get his employee out of jail, he would sign a bond that he would guarantee the fine would be paid and get his employee out to go to work. This was quite good for the city in that it was a good way to get money instead of the men lying in jail. Walter also instituted a procedure where a person in jail could volunteer to work on the garbage truck and be paid $3 per day toward his fine. This also was good, as it saved the city some $10,000 per year.

One particular incident brought to the court was that of two council persons, both of whom owned an auto agency, were caught speeding eighty or ninety miles per hour in the city limits early on Sunday morning. They both appeared in court and their pleas were guilty. Walter fined them each $100 and they stormed out of the courtroom. The police asked him as judge if they should be brought back, but Walter said they would be back on their own and pay the fine. At 11:00 a.m., they came in together and paid their fines.

The little house that Walter bought for his daughter and wife had two bedrooms, one bath, a living room with a fireplace, a nice kitchen and a small porch, which he converted to a breakfast room lined with knotty pines. The house also had a full walk-out basement, which housed a coal furnace for heat. The total cost again was $7,500 and the money came from the same bank at the same rate of interest. In 1949, gas was introduced to Lancaster and Walter had the coal furnace converted to gas, which was outstanding and easy to control, compared to feeding the furnace with coal. There was a large lot in the rear and he made a garden of corn, beans, tomatoes, okra, lettuce and other veggies. It was so large that he had to work hard and then share the crop with neighbors.

His brother, Glen and his wife lived up over the Miller funeral home since Glen was a mortician. The two brothers and families shared many meals together in each other's homes. One Saturday night, while at the funeral home, which had a large porch overlooking the front and opening by a door to the second floor, the city police came looking for Walter. They had a tourist in custody for exceeding the speed limit. Walter held court on porch with the tourist pleading guilty and levied a fine of $25 and let the man and his family go their merry way.

Another interesting time as police judge was a possible arrest of a man found with a body in his backseat of his car. The man was brought to Walter's office and was asked to tell about the body. The fellow said it was his sister and he had to bring her body from Tennessee to Ohio and he could not afford an ambulance. Walter procured the name of the funeral home where the lady was to be buried and phoned them to verify his story. It checked out and the culprit was warned to cover the body and not stop at any more towns along the way, as he might not get off so light. It was against the law to transfer a body in your private automobile.

On one occasion, Circuit Judge Kendrick Alcorn appointed Walter to be the attorney to locate unknown heirs in an estate case. There was $8,000 to be distributed to the two brothers who were somewhere in the United States unlocated. Walter went to work locating them and with the help of a company that specialized in that type of case, found the two men in St. Louis, Missouri. The judge allowed Walter a fee of $1,500, which was as much as he made the entire year other than that fee. Walter went to the Oldsmobile dealer and bought a new 1950 blue Oldsmobile with automatic transmission at a trade in value of $1,500. The car was two-door, light blue and the latest design, so Walter finally had the car of his dreams.

Since Walter was president of the Kiwanis Club and city judge, he was asked to head up the Red Cross Drive. He accepted and went to work collecting money for the Red Cross. It was hard to get money from people at that time because the economy had not improved that much since the war. He raised $3,000 plus and when the accounting was summed up, he found that the money was all used to pay a lady to be the head of the organization and rent for her office. None of the money was used to help any needy person.

One time, Mary Lee and Walter decided to travel to London to see Mary Lee's family. Old Highway 25 was a winding highway and the route through McKee, Kentucky, by way of Berea was less traveled and thus they tried that way. Just before the trip, it rained a lot; and when they went through McKee, they ran into a river on the road. It seems as if the high water had risen in that area and had covered the entire road for a distance of a few miles. They traveled back to McKee and on to old Highway 25 through Crab Orchard but found it to be impassible and then on to Somerset on old Highway 27 through Stanford, Kentucky and then on to London. Jeannie was a baby and it took all day long for that ninety-mile trip, which turned into a 150-mile trip.

During this time, his brother, Glen and his wife, Elizabeth Gulley Cox, gave birth to a baby girl. They named her Peggy

Lou or Margaret Louise Cox. She and her husband Billy Sharp live in Lancaster on the farm, which was owned by Cox Sr. He gave her an acre on which she and Billy built a very nice home. They have a daughter JAMIE who is married and has one daughter named Olivia. She only weighed 3 lbs when born and was kept in an incubator at the Hospital for several weeks. Walter and Pam visited the baby and held her in their hands, she was so small. She is now 4 years old and is a healthy young lady.

During this time of practice of law in Lancaster, Kentucky, the city built a Hospital. Walter was asked to be on the board of governors and when the grand opening took place, he sat on the podium with the county judge, county attorney and other dignitaries

In the fall of 1950, Gilbert Wilson, a fellow lawyer, phoned him and asked him if he had opened the mail. In hearing that he had not, Gilbert proceeded to tell him that he and Gilbert were on orders to report to active duty from the reserves. They both had reserve JAGC commissions and at that time, the military had developed new laws requiring all judges, prosecutors and defense persons to be lawyers. About 100,000 were called up for the military, as Korea was being fought and many divisions were deployed. Walter, with Mary Lee, reported to Fort Knox for a physical and left Jeannie at home with his mother, Blanche.

Jeannie & Walter   Walter & Jeannie

When Walter and Mary Lee returned they found Jeannie was sick so Dr Kinnard was called in to see her and the doctor determined it to beas the flue and gave her some medicine. The next day, she was worse and running a high fever, so Dr. Warfield (a pediatrician) in Lexington was called and he ordered her brought to him immediately. Mary Lee drove while Walter held Jeannie in the backseat. When they arrived, Dr. Warfield gave her a large shot of penicillin and put her in the isolation ward at the St. Joseph Hospital, saying she had spinal meningitis. For sixteen days, she was there and so was Walter with her at all times. She had to take a lot of pills and suppository medicine, which contained penicillin and the nurses would come in at night, wake them up and give the pills, etc. Of course, she recovered and on the last day, Walter blocked the door and when the nurse came to give her the pills, he told Jeannie no more pills and flushed them downs the commode. Jeannie was only three and a half years of age, but she was smart and knew about all the sickness she had. Jeannie lost the hearing on one ear, but otherwise, she recovered. It seems that their Baptist church prayed for her every night she was in the hospital and the Walter's angel worked again.

A JAGC and Korea

During that time, the military gave an extension for Walter to report to duty because of Jeannie's illness, but in January, the family had to report for duty and they made the move to Fort Knox and were assigned to the Wherry Housing project, which was built especially for returning veterans. The two-story apartment was very clean and new. It had two bedrooms on the second floor and a kitchen, bath and dining-living room on the first floor. There was no air-conditioning and the airport was very near, so the planes noise was a problem getting used to. In the summer, it was so hot the windows were left open and the planes taking off and landing were extremely noisy.

Walter on Trip To Korea

Walter was assigned to claims and to defense duty with JAGC and went to work every day at 8:00 a.m. to 5:00 p.m. He was assigned a case to defend a soldier who was a young recruit. He was charged with a homosexual act with a sergeant. Walter obtained letters from everyone in the boy's hometown and with a little persuasion about how young he was and was obeying the orders of a sergeant, the court found him not guilty.

The next day, the colonel called Walter in and reassigned him to the prosecutor's office and from then on, he was the prosecutor.

After four months of assignment at Fort Knox, the military sent Walter to Fort Myers, Virginia, for six weeks of training in the new military code. He was assigned to a group consisting of new lieutenants younger than he was. As a captain, wearing a combat infantry badge with other medals and being twenty-nine years old, it was natural for the other officers to look up to him. He was invited to weekends with the families of the other officers and went on a cruise near Annapolis with a family. All the time he was there, he visited all the sights in DC—the Smithsonian, the art museum, the Whitehouse, the Supreme Court, the Senate, the Mint and many others. The officers played volleyball and while playing the game, Walter sprained his ankle, which proceeded to swell twice its normal size. He had a hard time walking to class, but after three weeks, he was back to normal.

The officers teaching the classes told him that with his background in the War II, he would not ever go to Korea. When the duty was finished and Walter returned home to Fort Knox, within a week, orders were received, sending him to Korea. He moved Mary Lee and Jeannie to London to stay with Mary Lee's sister, Daisy and Cecil Yeary. He was sent just before Christmas 1951 on the trip to Seattle, Washington, en route to Japan and

Korea. He left Lexington on a train at the Southern station to Chicago and changed in Chicago to the Vista Vision train named Hiawatha. It had glass tops so you could look out at the mountains and snow. On arriving in Butte Montana, the passengers debarked in the sunshine to get a little stretching. It seemed a little cold and upon being told the temperature was twenty below zero, they all got back on to the train.

Walter on train to Seattle, Wash

Arriving in Seattle, Washington at Fort Lawton, he was taken to camp and assigned to a room in the officers' quarters and was quite surprised to find that his roommate was a lieutenant of the African American race. It was the first time Cox had ever had anything like that happen because never in War II or law school or as a lawyer had he ever had any professional contact with an African American. The officer, who happened to be a first

Walter in Seattle

lieutenant, was a gentleman and they both found the arrangement to be very compatible.

While Walter was waiting for shipment to Japan, he decided to have an impacted wisdom tooth extracted. The dentist on the base was of the old school apparently and after sedation of the jaw, proceeded to chisel the tooth from the socket. The dentist actually took an instrument, inserted it in the tooth and with a hammer, proceeded to break the tooth in pieces. The pieces were then extracted from the jaw. Within a few days, the jaw started swelling and hurting, but Walter was on orders to fly to Japan in a couple of days. During a dinner at the officers' club, the general's wife saw Walter, then a captain, with the swollen jaw and approached him, inquiring what was going on. When she heard the story, she called a doctor and had him look Walter over. He immediately started some shots for the problem and gave Walter some codeine to take every three hours. Before the three hours were gone, the pain was terrible and Walter looked forward each three hours to taking another pill. This was taking place in an infirmary where they put Walter and it was occupied by patients with rear-end cysts. The doctors would come in every morning and all patients would go to the end of their beds and bend over as the doctor looked over their rear ends. Walter would go to the head of his bed and point to his mouth when the doctor came to his bed. The orders to go to Japan were cancelled because of Walter's condition and reordered two weeks later so that he could go by ship instead of by air. The condition healed and Walter was ordered to Japan by way of a ship.

Walter found himself appointed the ship's communication officer in charge of a daily newspaper, which was distributed to all the men each day. He obtained his information from the communication which was sent by teletype and by radio. It was an exciting thing to do since he had never had any training or experience at such an undertaking. He had the run of the ship and again as he had in the trips to Europe and back, had to explore each compartment and engine room. The trip took about a week and was a very relaxing one. Walter read five books while doing the duty that had been assigned to him in addition to seeing all that could be seen of the boat.

Upon arriving in Tokyo, he again was assigned to quarters and the very next morning was summons to the JAG office in downtown. The colonel in charge made him an offer. He would be promoted to major and could stay in Tokyo and bring Mary Lee and Jeannie over to live. He only had to sign up for three years longer and he would stay in Japan. Walter told them he could not accept the offer and of course, the rest is history he was off to Korea. In two days, he was on a train to Saesbo, Japan, which was on the west coast of Japan and across from Pusan, Korea. The train was small and the seats were narrow and hard. *Unusual* is the word for the Japanese train. Upon arriving at Saesbo, he was immediately assigned to a boat for transportation to Pusan. He went to his quarters on the boat and it was very primitive, having straw ticks for mattresses and a couple of bunks. He chose the prime bunk and soon a major arrived. Walter offered the major the choice of bunks but the Major was nice and took the remaining one.

The night trip was over in a hurry and upon arrival in Pusan, all the troops were sent to a train to be transported to the front line. On the way up toward the line between North and South Korea, they were warned that an attack on the train could take place and to be prepared. The train arrived in the city of Taegu and a list of men was called off for those who would proceed to the front. If your name was not called, you would debark the train and be taken to headquarters. It was a tense time because his MOS was on his record as 1542, which was infantry leader. Walter's name was not called, so he got off the train and was met by his former fellow officers from Fort Knox. They welcomed him and took him to Jag Headquarters, where he met with Colonel Lancefield, who had been the chief JAG officer at Fort Knox. Colonel Lancefield told Walter that since he had been contacted by Mary Lee and the fact that he had been in combat in War II as an infantryman, he would return to Pusan and the Twenty-second Logistical Command. What a relief! (Angel.) That was as far South as you could be sent away from the fighting forces in Korea.

Walter was assigned to the headquarters, along with about twenty-two other lawyers who would be reviewing general courts-martial and other duties. They were quartered in a Quonset hut with individual rooms for two and common showers.

Quonset Hut

The place was comfortable and was cleaned daily by Korean women. The location of the hut was in the center of the horse race course located at Pusan and in the inside of the track was the clubhouse where the officers took their meals. So far so good. The meals were fairly good and in addition, the group had a bar where they gathered at each night to socialize and sing. Sometimes they would all go walking around the track, singing and telling jokes. In the compound, there was a dark room for developing film, so Walter learned how to develop his own film and proceeded to take a lot of pictures of Korea.

The duty assigned to him was reviewing the legality of general courts-martial and the written account of the trial. He had to

Walter in Pusan Law Office

read over the entire record, review the findings and also determine whether there was an error in the proceedings, rulings of the judge and other determinations. This was done expeditiously and soon Walter was called in to the colonel in charge of the unit and told he was assigned to Major Davis for further instructions. Major Davis told Walter that the procedure was to arrive at the office at eight o'clock each morning by bus from the billet. He was told to open his personal mail and to write home and to other relativesand then he would read the *Stars and Stripes* newspaper, read the bulletins from the headquarters and then by that time, go to the Red Cross for Donuts and coffee. About 10:00 a.m., he would then pick up his file to review and work on it meticulously for about forty-five minutes. At 11:00 a.m., he would meet with other officers and talk over the cases. At 12:00 p.m., they would all proceed to go to the mess hall for lunch. About 1:30 p.m., they would return to the office and confer with the staff about procedure. About 2:30 p.m., he would return to his file, further review the evidence, etc. At 3:15 p.m., they would all proceed to the Red Cross for coffee or to the hospital ship on the dock for ice cream. The ship was a large hospital ship that had accommodations for over one thousand wounded vets and had every known modern medical facilities. The most wonderful part of the Hospital ship was the ice cream.

After that and about 4:00 p.m., he would return to the office and pick up his file to further review it. For about an hour, he would work and then at 5:00 p.m., it was time to return to the billet at the racetrack. The reason was to slow down the process, which of course he was able to do the work of four or five of the lawyers and they did not like that because the empire they had built would fall down if everyone did their work eight hours a day, seven days each week. I suppose that is army style and Cox was not about to change it. About five attorneys were all they needed and they had twenty-two.

The length of time left in Walter's army time was only seven months out of the total of nineteen months, so it was just abide his time and eventually go home. During any off time, Walter spent exploring South Korea. The group of lawyers climbed the hills and took pictures. They went off to a Cherry Blossom Festival in another area, which was a beautiful island decorated with cherry trees. They followed a funeral up a hill, where the corpse was transported sitting upright by the pall bearers and then buried sitting up, with the dirt piled high to cover the entire sitting body. All draped in White and covered from toe to head, the body was buried that way without a casket. At Easter, there was a sunrise service high upon a hill at daybreak. The entire contingent decided to go and on that Sunday morning, with the sun shining over a hill, the setting was perfect for the service. There was a problem because there were refugees in tents all the way to the service location and upon arising, the refugees apparently decided to defecate at the same time and the smell was unbearable. The service was very short. Another time, when the bucket brigade came to the office to empty the septic tank, the smell was even worse so all the officers would leave for a time.

Walter went to the ocean close to the hospital ship and watched the Koreans fish. They had a line with several hooks and a little red ribbon on each hook. When thrown in the ocean, several fish would bite at the line with the hooks and the Korean fisherman would throw the pole back over his head with five or six fish attached. This would go on until the ground behind the fisherman would be filled with fish. These fish were a foot or more long and nice-looking.

While in Korea, Walter observed on the list of officers (Lieutenant General Thomas Herren), who was listed as a commanding officer of another unit but located in Pusan. This General was the same one who was a brigadier general when he commanded Task Force Herren for Walter's 274th Infantry Regiment at the first combat in France at Christmas 1944. It was he who was in charge of the battle of Wingen and was the General who came up behind Walter while Walter was lying in a ditch. Walter called him on the phone and reminded him of that particular part of the action and General Thomas Herren invited Walter to come see him. The reunion was one of highlights of the duty in Korea. Tom (General Herren) recalled all the events in Wingen and laughed when reminded of his foolhardy move to the edge of Wingen that winter night of 1945.

While Walter was in Korea and had free time, there would be some fun-filled days such as a party at the club. Walter was in charge of going to the supply food depot and procuring all kinds of delicacies for the party. He would obtain cans of cheese, ham, turkey, crackers, chips and other tasty items for the party.

Everyone in the section would gather on a Friday or Saturday night and drink beer and eat the tidbits.

The duty in Korea consisted of another special honor. All the officers who were lawyers and in the Twenty-second Logistical

Command applied for and were granted admission to the Korean Bar. They were hosted by the law department of the Korean government and given official admission, allowing them to practice law in Korea.

One particular case that Walter reviewed told about a sergeant in a medical unit who was found using drugs. It stated that he had a sore on his forearm about the size of a silver dollar. When the sergeant needed a fix, he would pour the drug as a powder into the open wound. Walter interviewed all the prisoners by having them brought to the office. When this sergeant was brought in to find out if he had any defense to his conviction, Walter asked

Walter in Korea

Walter being given admission to Korean Bar

him to expose his arm where the open wound had been. The scar was larger than a silver dollar and there it was as sure as it was related at the trial. Walter asked him about how it happened. The sergeant told him all about trying it out after he had an open wound on his arm and then he was hooked on the drug but that now he was off it and never again hooked.

After August 1952, Walter received orders to return home from duty in Korea. Once again, on a cargo ship from Pusan to Saesbo, Japan and then by train to Tokyo and sailed out of Tokyo on a ship for San Francisco. On this trip, Walter was assigned the duty as military police and again had the run of the ship. Going home was interesting because each day, the time would change an hour and soon when bedtime at 11:00 p.m. came, it was in reality only 6:00 p.m. and no one could go to sleep. All night long, the officers would crack jokes, talk, play poker, shoot craps, or just talk until about 6:00 a.m. and then fall asleep and sleep until noon. It was very different than going over, as that was just the reverse and you would fall asleep at 6:00 p.m., about the time you arrived in Tokyo.

Just as the ship was going under the Golden Gate Bridge, the waves were really terrible and everyone was getting seasick. The ship was going from side to side and almost dipped water at the first level before rocking back on the other side. Walter stood on the outside of the top deck and watched the horizon and even though the ship was rocking heavily, he never got seasick; in fact, he had never been seasick on any trip by ocean. When the ship docked and all the men were put on buses and taken to the camp, Walter got sick and stuck his head out the window of the bus to get rid of his breakfast.

After a couple of days, the group being separated from the service were boarded on the train in San Francisco, headed toward Chicago and home.

Attorney Second Time Around

It was the end of the second tour of duty for Walter and he was glad to get home in August 1952. Mary Lee again met him in Lexington, Kentucky and this time, they spent a few days at the New Campbell House that had been built that year out on Harrodsburg Road. They danced every night and had a great time touring Lexington and seeing some of their friends. After that, the couple went to London, where Jeannie was staying with her aunt Daisy (Mary Lee's sister) and uncle Cecil Yeary, who was married to Daisy. Jeannie was born March 24, 1947, only nine months to the day after Walter arrived home from Europe and the World War II, so she now was five years old. She was ecstatic seeing Walter for the first time since before Christmas 1951. It was a wonderful reunion for them both and they loved every minute and every day for a long time. Mary Lee had already contacted a couple she knew and had rented a nice cottage with two bedrooms and a bath and had moved in.

Mary Lee's family had a business known as the London Grocery Company, which was a partnership owned by the family. Mary Lee's sister, Edna, was married to Fred Byble and it was he who was the manager of the business and had been since

Mary Lee's father was killed in an accident in 1939. It seems that Mr. Engle, while working at the Grocery Company jumped on the back of a truck to go to the railroad and load groceries being shipped to the wholesale grocery company. As they crossed the tracks, the truck threw Mr. Engle off and his head was injured and he soon died. Mary Lee was the first to reach him as he lay on the ground bleeding and she never got over that accident.

Fred Byble had suffered a heart attack and it was not known whether he could continue to be the manager of the business. Since there was no other member of the family to take over, Walter was approached with the idea of working and learning the business so he could take over in the event Fred Byble did not recover from the heart attack and had to step out of the management. Walter accepted and he and Mary Lee lived in the rented cottage and he went to work learning all about the grocery business.

The apprenticeship consisted of learning to buy, learning to sell, loading trucks, delivering groceries to the stores and generally everything about the day to day operation of the grocery wholesale business. There were five salespersons who called on twenty stores each or approximately 100 stores every day, making a grand total of 500 customers for wholesale groceries. Each of the trucks would load the following day with orders taken the day before and deliver to the twenty stores that had placed orders. So with five trucks and twenty stores each, the trucks delivered to 100 stores each day. In order to learn the entire route, Walter went with each salesman for his entire route and found out where these 500 stores were located and the route that the salesman would follow each day. Some times the salesmen were busy and Walter had to run his route. On the trips especially to Hyden, a small town in the mountains, there would be coal trucks coming toward him on the wrong side of the road. Walter would stop and the trucks would finally turn to the proper side of the road to get around the stopped car. The roads were so beat up with the coal trucks weighing 20 tons that the truckers used the opposite side of the road which was in better condition. All along the road, there would be burned out hulks of trucks burned down to the metal frame. Walter found out that when a truck quit running, the owner would set it on fire to collect the insurance. Obviously the hulk would be left in place on the side of the road. It was amazing to him that such a thing could happen.

After that learning curve, he went with every grocery truck to find out just how efficient the truck drivers were in delivering the groceries to the stores. The payments for the groceries would be paid to the salesman when he called on the store and took new orders. The truckers would get signed delivery slips after delivering to the stores. It all worked very well, but Walter went further and checked on the loading procedures of the truck drivers; Walter would just hop on a truck and go with the trucks to check and see if any illegal loading of groceries may have been taking place. He found that sometimes a case of canned goods or a bag of feed or more would remain on the truck, indicating that someone was putting extra merchandise on the trucks to be taken off before returning to the company. Walter put a stop to that and fired some of the help. In order to further the procedure, Walter would be a checker when the trucks were being loaded to further the detective work and cut down on theft.

After two years of this type of work and learning all that could be learned, it was determined that Fred Byble was completely recovered and would continue to manage the company. Mary Lee and Walter decided to leave and go to Lexington, Kentucky, where Walter would enter the practice of law.

It was the fall of 1954 and after a week-long search of a house to buy, an offer was made on 1189 Indian Mound. The house as new, had three bedrooms, two bathrooms and a two-car garage, with no basement and was featured as an all-electric home. The offer was $26,000 on a house listed by the builder for $35,000 and was set to terminate at midnight on Saturday. At 11:00 p.m., F. D. Kindred, the builder, called and said he should not do it because he was being taken advantage of, but he accepted the offer. Since that time, the builder and Walter became friends and each were reminded of that offer and purchase back in 1954. (By the way, this house is now listed at $400,000.)

Walter searched all week for employment as a lawyer and was turned down by everyone. They all told him that there were too many lawyers in Lexington. He finally found Tommy Bell in the old Citizens Union National Bank, who had County Judge Dan Fowler's office for rent, as Judge Dan E. Fowler had just been elected County Judge for Fayette County. He rented the office for $100 per month and started his law practice in September 1954. Tom Bell and Walter had been in basic training in the infantry. Tommy Bell later on became the NFL football referee who eventually was the referee at the first NFL game played in Minnesota with the temperature at zero. He later refereed almost every weekend. Prior to that, he also was a NBA referee. Tom Bell was probably the most recognized official of the NBA and NFL at any one time in his career.

The Cox family moved from London to Lexington and six-year-old daughter Jeannie was enrolled in the first grade at Julia R. Ewan School. Mary Lee went about getting the house in order and Walter went to work, practicing law. The first thing he had to do was get admitted to the Courts in Lexington, State and Federal. Then get introduced to the clerks, judges, magistrates and other officials. Walter told everyone around the courthouse, including lawyers, that he needed clients and if they had anyone who they could not represent or if there was a conflict, to send them to him. Tommy Bell had a few clients and cases he shared with Walter and soon the practice was going full tilt. In a few months, he was busy and he and Tommy formed a partnership called "Bell and Cox Law Firm." It was the start of the law firm where Walter retired in 1988

One case that Tommy and Walter had involved a man adopting his wife to enable the wife to inherit from the husband's trust fund. The trust stated that after the death of the husband, all money would be distributed to his children. The fellow had no children; therefore, he adopted his wife as his child so she could inherit the balance of the trust fund. Walter represented the heirs of the estate who would inherit if there were no children of the man. Judge Adams, who was married but had no children, ruled the adoption to be legal and the wife could inherit. Tommy and Walter appealed the case to the Court of Appeals and the court voted four to three in favor of the adoption. The Court of Appeals reversed the ruling in another case approximately three or four years after that and the decision is standing to this day. However, Bell and Cox got nothing in fees.

This firm was fairly successful and soon Darrell Hancock was taken in as a third partner and the firm was named "Bell, Cox and Hancock." This law firm continued until Judge Dan E. Fowler came back to the firm in 1957, after serving as County Judge for four years and again the firm's name was changed to Fowler, Bell, Cox and Hancock. The firm did fairly well and continued as such for several years. In 1959, the firm merged with Stiltz, Rouse and Measle and again the firm was renamed Fowler, Rouse, Measle and Bell, the group consisting of Dan E. Fowler, Robert Measle, Arthur Rouse, Thomas P. Bell, Walter Clay Cox Jr. and Darrell B. Hancock, with Tom Collins and Grover Thompson as associates.

The partners all decided they would have meetings for dinner at various hotels once each month. Sometimes the idea was to discuss procedure of running a law firm and other times it consisted of discussing cases of interest that no one knew about on a regular basis. The meetings sometime got out of hand and some drinking may have caused the problems. One particular time, after Walter had been office manager for a month or so (each lawyer took three months at a time being office manager), he was criticized by Bell. Walter came out of his chair with his fists ready and challenged Bell to a fight. Of course, all the others stepped in and prevented any blows to be struck. It was funny afterward and Walter and Tommy never had any words after that episode. Sometime later, Arthur Rouse withdrew from the firm and the name was changed to Fowler, Measle and Bell. (It is now Fowler Bell as of July 2012.)

Married Life and Second Daughter

During this period and May 9, 1957, Rebecca Lee Cox was born, with the same doctor, Dr. Whitehouse and in the same hospital as Jeannie's delivery. Mary Lee had a difficult delivery, which lasted twenty-four hours. Becky, was so beautiful when presented to Walter and she looked like a doll with black hair and with a chubby face as pretty as a picture. The nurses tied her hair with a ribbon when they brought her out to the waiting room. She was ten years younger than Jeannie and therefore became a play thing for the ten-year-old Jeannie.

Walter Jeannie Dad Becky

The best thing that happened during the first three or so weeks was the hiring of a black lady who took care of new babies and mothers. She lived in the home, cooked and took Becky with her into her room at night and Becky was quiet as a mouse. Becky did not cry at night and the habit formed early in her life was the thing she carried with her until now. During Becky's growing era, the family lived at 1189 Indian Mound Road in Lexington until she was about two and a half years of age and then a new home was built at 537 Clinton Road, not far from the home they sold. The new home was a duplicate of one that was featured on the front page of the *American Home* magazine and was built in Seattle Washington, overlooking the bay. It had and still has large open windows in the living room, overlooking Clinton and Prather roads, which are below the site of the home. The home was designed to have the living room and dining room as one large room separated by steps up to the dining area and to the entrance hall. The kitchen had a fireplace, as did the living room and basement. There was room for an eat-in-kitchen and a television. Also off this area, there was a half bath with a laundry drop to the wash room below. This part was separated from the four bedrooms by a hallway from the front door to the rear door. The master bedroom had a large bath and the other three bedrooms had a large bath at the end of the hall, which separated the three bedrooms from the master suite.

Off the center hallway, there was a stairway down to the partial finished basement. There was a bedroom and a bath in addition to a recreation room with a bar and refrigerator and fireplace. Then, of course, there was the laundry room, which housed the furnace, water heater and washer and dryer also.

One night, while Walter and Mary Lee were watching TV at about ten thirty, some noise was heard outside in the front of the home. Walter went to the picture window and observed men tearing down mail boxes and house markers. The area was perfect because Clinton and Prather roads met at the corner and on down Prather Road, there was a dead-end street. Walter told the police that if they came down both streets, they would pin the culprits in and could catch them. That is exactly what happened and as Walter was watching, the police drove to the car and the bad guys ran up into the yard of one of the houses. The dog that lived at that house was a Weirmanier and it chased them right down to the police car and they jumped in the backseat of the police car.

Another time, someone stole the house marker, which was an iron post with a horse's head on top. One night after that event, Jeannie was babysitting a house on Bristol Road when she looked in a station wagon parked at the house and observed their house marker in the back of the wagon. She told Walter who had the marker and Walter contacted the boy's mother and told her what had been found. The mother told Walter he could do what he wanted. Walter contacted the boy, who incidentally lived across the street on Clinton Road and informed him that he was to meet Walter with the marker and some concrete. Walter had him dig a hole, put the marker in the hole and fill the hole with concrete. The boy was glad he was not reported to the police. Thereafter, many times, the man (culprit) thanked Walter for teaching him a lesson by making him put the marker back in the yard.

Walter's Mom

In 1961, Blanche Marie Phillips Cox, Walter's mom became ill. Walter and Mary Lee insisted she come to Lexington to be examined. The doctor discovered she had cancer of the bowel and that it was so large and spread to other organs that the only remedy was to take out the tumor and put in a colostomy which consisted of a bag for her bowel. She remained at home with Walter Sr. taking care of her for about a year. Walter was called when his dad had her taken to the local hospital. His dad could not stand to let her die at home, although she was down to eighty pounds from her normal weight of 160 pounds. When Walter went to the hospital, he ordered the lifesaving remedies removed and his mom died the next day. She is buried in the Lancaster cemetery, along with Walter Sr. and brother Glen.

Mom & Dad

The law practice was a changing factor from Walter's early start in 1948 until he retired in 1988 after forty years. The early years were using a manual typewriter, no copy machines (the only copier was at the County Clerk's Office and it took three days to get one copy), no air conditioner, no central heat (a coal oil stove in the middle of the room), a fan to keep cool and a wall phone. Walter ordered two phones, one for each desk, as Green Clay Walker and Walter used the same room as an office, which was equipped with the small library of law books, a couple of filing cabinets and lots of chairs. There was only an electric fan to keep cool and in the winter, there was an oil heater bought after Walter remodeled the office. Before that, it was a coal stove in the middle of the office to keep it warm. Walter had to carry oil up the stairs every morning to keep the stove going. Green Clay taught Walter all about the practice of law, how to type deeds, how to file a lawsuit, how to prepare income tax and how to handle clients and gave him instructions about looking busy when he went out on the street to go to the courthouse.

Walter went to school in Lexington to learn about income tax and it seems that Green Clay had a lot of clients who were farmers that needed taxes prepared. From the middle of January until the end of February, the clients would line up in the outer office and wait their turn to get tax returns filed. Walter would interview the client, put the tax forms in the manual typewriter, type in the figures, obtain checks to pay taxes and put the finished product in an envelope and give it to the client to mail. Of course, his fee would be collected at that time and generally, it was $10. Judge Walker and Walter shared in all those type fees.

After Walter relocated in Lexington after Korea, the electric typewriter was invented and was the most modern innovation yet. Then a copy machine, which was a wet copier, was introduced and was used a lot, but the paper would fade in about three months, so it was no good. In 1957, a copy machine was invented for the office that actually made copies on black and white regular paper.

Walter practiced law in the area of bankruptcy and after a couple of years, he made friends with an older attorney in Lexington by the name of Grover Thompson. Grover had been president of the Commercial Law League of America and he invited Walter to go to a national convention at French Lick Springs, Indiana. Grover, his wife, Walter and Mary Lee and daughter Jeannie went to the convention and enjoyed all the festivities. There Walter made more friends and joined the league. He now has fifty years in the league and is a life member (plaque). During those years, there were a lot of conventions and a lot of business was obtained by joining the Law Lists, where clients would

Life Member Plaque

use the listed lawyers and other members of the league would refer clients from other states and cities. Grover was active in bankruptcy, with a lot of claims against persons filing bankruptcy, so it was natural for Grover to have Walter appointed trustee in many of the bankruptcy cases since the lawyer who had claims could nominate the trustee. The trustee would be the person to bring all the assets from the bankrupt and dispose of them to be divided between the creditors. The trustee would receive a fee for each case.

One large case was the Baynham Shoe Store on Main Street in Lexington. Charles Rhodes married the daughter of the owner of Baynhams and was the manager when the store filed bankruptcy. Walter actually ran the store for two months, trying to sell as much of the merchandise at retail as he possibly could. After the final retail sale, the store and fixtures were sold at auction and Charles Rhodes was the buyer. Charley started another shoe store and ran it for a number of years until he sold out and became a realtor. Another large bankruptcy was a wholesale grocery company that had a store in central Ohio. Walter held an auction of this wholesale company and had to drive on the old Twenty-five Road from Lexington to Ohio and arrive by 8:00 a.m. That was the earliest he had to drive to sell a bankruptcy inventory. Later on, Walter saw fit to stay out of the trustee part and would buy assets of some of the cases. In one case, he bought a men's store and took it to his home and held a sale in the basement. There were shoes, clothes, racks, ties, shirts, underclothes and many other items too numerous to mention. Another time, he bought a women's store and did the same thing, only this time he was dealing with women customers. It was fun and profitable.

When Walter first started practicing in Lexington, it was normal for the judge to appoint a young lawyer to defend the criminals. At that time, there were no defense counsels paid by the state to represent the criminals as there are now. This particular case was set for 9:00 a.m. and it was a cold snowy morning in Lexington. Walter had to take daughter Jeannie to school across town and because of the snow and ice, was about five minutes late to the trial. As he walked in the courtroom before about 200 people, Judge Bradley announced to Walter that he had been keeping the court and about 200 bystanders in limbo because Walter was late. It was very demeaning to him and he never forgot it.

Walter, along with Tom Bell, was appointed to a case where a man had killed another man by shooting him six times. The case happened in Manchester, Kentucky and was transferred to Lexington because he could not get a fair trial in his home county. When Walter interviewed the accused, he found that this was the type of Hatfield and McCoy Feud.

The two men were shooting across a field from the top of one hill to another. The client was shot six times and he shot the dead one seven times. Walter asked his client to show the bullet wounds and his client took off his shirt and showed six wounds, each of which was not deadly, but nevertheless, they were holes in arms, shoulders and stomach and were very evident. At the trial, Tom Bell brought one of his suits, shirts and ties and dressed the accused so he looked really good. When he (the accused) was put on the stand, he told of being shot six times and asked to remove his clothes to show the jury and the wounds. The jury was very interested in that and, of course, found the guy not guilty by reason of self-defense.

One estate case that he never forgot and has told it to many clients involved a client who had to place her mother in a nursing home. The mother was there for over two years before she died. After the funeral, the daughter came to Walter's office, carrying a shoe box. She placed it on the desk and remarked, "I bet you do not know what this box contains." Walter said, "Open it and let's see." It was stuffed full of money, silver certificates and silver dollars and Walter asked her how much was in the box. Her reply was that she had not counted it. Walter cleaned off the desk and they counted more than $60,000 and this was in 1960. He asked his client if she had searched the entire house and she said she had not. Walter, wanting to be helpful, asked her if she needed help in searching. She replied that she thought her husband and she would be able to do it. For three days, the client kept coming in with additional shoeboxes and in the final count, there was over $300,000 in various forms of currency and silver. It seems that the family had a plot of land behind their home, which they used for growing flowers and vegetables. Her mother sold the merchandise and kept all the cash without anyone knowing about it and this had been going on here in Lexington, Kentucky, since 1900. The client declared the money and paid taxes on the windfall in the estate.

GLEN WALLACE COX

Walter's brother became a funeral director and mortician in Lancaster and worked with Mr. (Twenty) Miller, who owned the Miller Funeral Home. He married Elizabeth Gulley and Walter was best man at the wedding, which took place at the home of Elizabeth. Glen and Elizabeth had one daughter named Peggy Lou, who was born about a year after Jeannie was born. They lived in Lancaster and many times, the public would mistake Glen for Walter and asked when a case was set for trial and asked Walter when a funeral was to be held. They looked that much alike and were about the same size. Glen and Elizabeth moved in with Walter Sr. after Blanche died in 1962. Blanche had kept Peggy Lou while she was young since both Glen and Elizabeth worked. Glen did not stay in the funeral business but did mortician work all over Kentucky. He died in 1972 and Peggy Lou and Elizabeth continued to live in the home with Walter Sr. until maybe ten years later when Elizabeth married Cecil Sanders, an attorney in Lancaster. Cecil Sanders graduated from law school at the University of Kentucky in February before Walter graduated in August of 1947. Cecil taught school in Lancaster High School at the time when Walter was attending the same school. Cecil served in the navy during World War II and was commander of a PT boat in the Pacific. During his service, he met and became friends with President Kennedy. Cecil was also City Attorney during the time that Walter was City Judge.

More of Life and as a Law Partner

Walter had a black man named Lloyd who helped around his home doing chores such as cutting grass, cleaning windows—odd jobs of all kinds. Lloyd was very loyal and would come at any time to help out, except when he was on a drunk. He usually advanced money to Lloyd because he begged so much when he would need money for booze. One instance, Walter came out of his office and there sat Lloyd at the bottom of the steps. He followed Walter to the courthouse and was saying, "Mr. Cox, aren't you ashamed to have a nigger following you to the courthouse?" He was wanting more money and Walter would not give him any more. Walter had a case in the courtroom and when he came out and went back to the office, he had phone calls from five different people who were located along the route from the courthouse all the way to the jail. It seems that Lloyd was lying half drunk and asleep outside the courtroom where Walter was trying a case and when the jailer went by him with some prisoners who were being taken back to the jail, he just hooked Lloyd onto the chain with all of them. On the way to the jail, Lloyd kept telling everyone, "Call, Mr. Walter Cox and tell him that Lloyd is in jail and he should come and get me out."

Lloyd was loyal but he always kept ahead with money. He would get an advance, get drunk and then when he sobered he would come and ask for work. He would then work for a week or two and then get drunk again. Never in all the time he worked for Walter was he ever dishonest.

Another funny thing happened after Easter when Becky was given a little baby chick. It was fed for two months and grew to be a nice chicken. It was given to Lloyd to take home and to kill and eat. Becky cried so much that Lloyd could not stand it and he brought the chicken back home. It was finally disposed of to another family.

Another funny thing happened at a birthday party for Becky. One of Walter's friends brought a pony to the party for everyone to ride. It was tethered in the backyard of the home and after the party, there was no one to take it back to the farm, so it was left in the yard. The next morning, somehow the pony escaped and ran up the street with all of the family trying to catch it. It took about two hours to corner it in someone's yard, but it was caught. The pony was taken back to the farm and never seen again.

The family dog was called Tammy and was a little rat terrier dog that weighed about eight pounds. She was taken everywhere and was a great pet for the entire family. When she finally died, she was buried in a suitcase in the side yard of the property at 537 Clinton Road. After Walter sold the house in 1976, Becky visited the house and told the new owners that her dog was in their side yard.

Becky had a cat that was really mobile. It would climb the draperies and when Becky would walk down the hall, the cat would jump on Becky and scare her. Obviously, the cat did not stay long.

One Christmas, Jeannie received a box as large as a refrigerator carton all wrapped in tissue paper. When she opened it, she found another wrapped box inside; and upon opening it, she found another and this went on through about twenty boxes. The final one was a little box which contained a piece of jewelry. It seems that Pat Moore was the guy who sent it. He worked for our law firm and was attending college. Pat went on to finish college and then was inducted into the army during Vietnam. After that, he went to law school and became an attorney with the firm of Fowler, Measle and Bell. He went on to become a partner in the firm and now is in the individual practice.

To enhance his practice of law, Walter joined the Kiwanis Club, Calvary Baptist Church, Lexington Country Club, the Lexington Club and the Civil War Roundtable and was active in all of them, becoming president of Kiwanis, Sunday school teacher, usher at Calvary, vice president of Lexington Country Club and secretary of the Fayette County Bar Association. He and Mary Lee joined the Cotillion Dance Club and attended many dances over the years. She was a member of the Lexington Woman's Club and raised a lot of money for it by procuring advertising for the play that they put on every year.

Every year the family would go to Florida during spring break. One year, when Becky was two and a half years old and the Southern rail company was removing the only train that ran out of Lexington, Walter reserved a Pullman car to Daytona Beach, Florida. The entire family, Jeannie, Becky, Mary Lee and Walter boarded the train and set off for the trip. In Atlanta, the Pullman was attached to the train and the family had beds for everyone to sleep on through the night to Daytona. Upon arrival in the morning and when breakfast was over in the dining room, the trip was finished and the vacation at Daytona began. It was the same returning to Lexington and that was the last time a train trip took everyone to Florida.

In 1962, Walter's mother, Blanche developed colon cancer and was operated on at the Central Baptist Hospital. It was a tumor about the size of an orange and had spread throughout her body. There was little they could do but make her comfortable and she stayed home in Lancaster for about one year before she finally passed away. She never complained about anything and was the calmest person you could ever meet. She kept a diary from the time she was a teenager until she died and in notebook form. Needless to say, there are hundreds of the notebooks of every day of her life. Blanche loved the movies and love stories and played the piano by ear. She entertained everyone on the street with her music and, in addition, played the piano and organ at the Lancaster Baptist church all her life in Lancaster. She played for the silent movies during the 1916 era until 1927, when talking movies came about. She would play a lively tune if there was action and a slow tune if there was romance.

Blanche was a seamstress using a Singer sewing machine that ran when you pedaled it with your feet. She made clothes for Walter, especially when he was in plays at the Lancaster School. There were plays where the costume had to be pantaloons or knickers and vests and ruffles. In the last play, Walter was a lawyer in the Senior Play and wore a hat and carried a briefcase. He played against the popular Mary Ruth Wilburn, who was supposed to kiss Walter, but it was never done until the night of the play when Walter did kiss her and she could not object because it was on the stage in front of all the school and parents. Blanche took Walter and Glen to church every Sunday and Reverend Gabbert was the preacher.

Again thinking back about growing in Lancaster

Walter and Billy Gabbert were best friends in school and in church. They sat together and read the Sunday school bulletin every Sunday. One incident that involved Billy was a day when he told Walter about going home from school sick and when he went in the front door, he encountered his mother and the reverend naked on the couch. Walter never forgot that when he listened to the sermon every Sunday thereafter. He would visualize the reverend and his wife naked. The prohibitions that Reverend Gabbert preached were numerous. They were to never drink liquor, never go to movies on Sunday, never dance and many others which would surely send you to hell. The preacher would depict what hell would be like. He said you would be in boiling oil right up to your mouth and nose and that you would be there for eternity. He would rant and rave and get red in the face and yell so loud that Walter wanted to put his hands on his ears.

Walter went to Sunday school and church every Sunday and sometimes helped his mother by turning the music as she played. The church had a youth program, but Walter did not like it, so he went to the Epworth League at the Methodist church to be with his friends. They had a young minister who was friendly and did not talk about Hell. The group would go to other churches in buses and have outings and parties. Reverend Green was also the scout master and active in the other events in Lancaster. During the first year as a tender foot scout, the scout master had the boys rassle in the grass located in the middle of town. Walter was teamed up with David Kinnard, as they were the same size. Walter was eleven and David twelve years of age. They rassled and rassled on the ground, but neither could pin the other to the ground. Finally, the event was called a draw.

Walter remembers that he was shaking and worn completely down to a frazzle. He remembers that he and the boys went to the soda fountain on the corner and drank Coke. While they were there, there was a machine that had two handles which you used to put both hands on and try to press them together all the time the machine was giving you a shock of electricity. Walter never forgot that the machine brought him back to his normal self doing away with the tired feeling he had after the boys had the rassling match.

Fast forward to law practice

In 1966, Charley Jett Jr. owned an appliance store (Jetts Appliances), whom Walter represented and he and Walter played golf at the Lexington Country Club. It seems that Jett had a lawyer named Tom Underwood, who represented him in suing a person who had bought an appliance and not paid for it. Walter was hired by the defendant to defend the lawsuit. The lawsuit ended up being dismissed and Mr. Jett was in Walter's office the very next morning. When Walter walked, in Charley announced that the appliance store would henceforth be represented by Walter. After that relationship in law, Walter also worked with Charley in forming the Appliance Dealers Better Business Bureau, which was joined by all the appliance dealers including PIERATTS, in Lexington, Kentucky, to keep the dealers from doing shady deals. Walter was the person people complained to and had to mediate their differences. This was about the same time the Better Business Bureau of Eastern Kentucky was formed in Lexington.

During the law practice in Lexington, Walter was active in the Fayette County Bar Association as the secretary of the group and then as in charge of the law library for a period of six years.

It was the lady who was hired to work in the law library that Walter hired to be his secretary at the law firm. Roberta MClure was from Mt. Vernon, Kentucky and was very timid. She was so efficient that once she learned about legal procedures, deeds, making wills and drawing up pleadings, she was perfect. Walter had many cases during that period of time, doing collection work in addition to real estate, trials, divorces, with a total of over one thousand cases being active at any one time. The secretary was Roberta McClure and she is now retired in Mt. Vernon.

During this entire time during Walter's practice of law in Lexington, consisting of commercial, bankruptcy, corporate, wills, deeds, divorces and trials for other related types of cases. He enjoyed going to the office every day because there was always a problem presenting itself that had to be solved. He always called himself a problem solver. The one thing that Walter always did and does to this day is answer every phone call he received during the entire day. He says that many lawyers in his own law firm would not answer their phone calls for two or three days.

One case involved a lady who had married a man in Texas and had two children. She and her husband were convicted of selling drugs and imprisoned. Her sentence was lighter than her husband's, so she was released and then came to Lexington, Kentucky. She came to see Walter and told him that her mother-in-law would not give her the two children who were now old enough to attend school. Walter found out where the children were attending school and advised the lady (client) to obtain plane tickets to Texas and go to the school and since she could prove she was the mother, take the children from school and go immediately to the airport and fly to Lexington, Kentucky. That being accomplished, the mother-in-law did nothing about it because she would have no chance in a Kentucky Court. The children grew up in Lexington and Walter hired the daughter when she was sixteen years of age to work after school hours under a program at Tates Creek School. In 2010, that same daughter, who was now fifty years of age, came to Walter's office and had a similar problem involving her mother-in-law, except she went to Georgia and brought her mother-in-law to Lexington, Kentucky to take care of. The husband's brother had placed the mother in a nursing home and it was against the advice of the brother (her husband), so upon Walter's advice, she traveled to Georgia, picked the mother-in-law up at the nursing home and brought her to Lexington to be with her husband and she is there to this day.

In the early years of Walter's practice in Lancaster and not having much income from his practice, his brother-in-law, Cecil Yeary, from London, Kentucky, told him to start an insurance agency. He procured one of his agents with USF&G Insurance Company and got his license and went into business. He advertised in the paper and at the local outdoor movie theater and the clients started coming in. At the end of the first six months, he had written $3,000 in business and the money was due. The agent from the company came and visited on the day the money was due and Walter wrote a check for the full amount. The commission was 20 percent, so Walter felt he was making real money to start with. This agency did real well and when Walter had to go to Korea, Walter Sr. took it over and ran it until his death in 1984.

In addition to the law practice, Walter was active buying and selling real estate. He would look for houses for sale in the newspaper, go to the seller and make offers. At the time, loans could be assumed and many ex-soldiers had GI loans with low interest rates but could not keep up the payments or were moving or getting a divorce or someone died. Walter would pay $1,000 down and assume the loan on the house. He would then clean and paint the home and resell it for $3,000 down and let the buyer assume the loan again. He probably bought and sold fifty houses in Lexington doing that procedure.

On one Sunday morning, while Walter was reading the Sunday paper he found a 400 acre farm for sale for $25000.00 It was located on I-75 North about 40 miles from Lexington, Walter drove to the house and bought the farm that Sunday morning. He sold it for $35,000 the following year and has regretted it every since. There were other farms bought in Franklin County, Scott County and Bourbon County and subdivided in 1 acre or less lots and sold on time with monthly payments. This and another farm in Bourbon County, on Cane Ridge road, consisting of 60 acres where a grandson was left the farm for his lifetime. Walter bought the lifetime interest and rented the farm for growing of tobacco and corn. The life owner lived from 1967 until 2009 giving Walter a farm 42 years of ownership and lots of profit for his $12,000.00 investment.

In 1967, Charley Jett talked Walter into vacationing at Captiva Island, Florida. It was the first time the family had gone to the west coast of Florida. Another attorney, Angus McDonald, had built a Michigan Home on the gulf and Charley Jett had built on the Bay both on the same strip of land that went all the way across the island. The two of them bought the entire lot from Gulf to Bay for the sum of $13,000. The McDonald house had three bedrooms with two baths and had a nice living room and kitchen and garage.

After the family arrived at the MCDONALD rental home and every day thereafter, Mary Lee went to the Gulf and collected shells. When it came time to go home, there were large boxes of sea shells that had to be fitted into the trunk of the automobile. Upon arrival home, shells were scattered all over the patio and were displayed in all sorts of jars. Everyone enjoyed the trip so much that it took place every year until Walter finally, in 1969, bought a lot on the island for $7,500. A friend, Boyd Deaton and law partner, Peter Perlman, all agreed to build a home on the lot. Boyd went down and actually cleared the lot with a machete, along with another fellow. He then built the house from the ground up from a plan almost like the house that belonged to McDonald. It had a bedroom and bath on one end, a living room in the middle and two bedrooms and a bath on the other end. It was made out of brick and it was the only one on the island constructed of brick.

That was in 1973-1974 and there was only one year that the family visited the island Walter. Becky took Janet Berry with her on the trip and in the middle of the night, they screamed that there were spiders all over the walls and ceiling. The spiders were large and were called housekeepers. Supposedly, they were harmless and kept the insects from invading a home. It was strange to see them all over the walls and ceiling, but they finally were disposed of without harm to anyone.

Becky Growing

One incident involving Becky when she was about fourteen years old, which occurred when Walter went to her room to check on she and Norma Taylor, who lived next door and was spending the night. He looked in at the room and it appeared they were in bed, but on checking closer, he found pillows stuffed in the bed to look like them. The window was unlocked and since the room was close to the ground, it was obvious that they had gone out the window. Walter waited outside the door until he heard them coming back in through the window and accosted them. They never did that again. Another famous incident was when Becky was fifteen years old and wanted to have a party in the recreation room in the basement. She invited several of her friends, but when they started coming, there were fifty or sixty that showed up and many were strangers. After putting up with it for a short period, Walter went to the basement and found a mess. The boys had beer and were spraying it everywhere and Becky was in the corner saying, "What am I going to do?"

Walter announced from the middle of the floor that everyone was to leave and they did leave, except personal friends of Becky, who stayed or came back. The next morning, there were beer cans, bottles and debris all over the lawn. Becky's parties were closely monitored from then on.

One trip to the Commercial Law League of America in New York City, Mary Lee and Walter had a three-day stay and then, along with some of the other attendees, flew to Spain for another week. It was a beautiful vacation. They visited all the small towns around Madrid and ate at the small restaurants in the villages. There was another couple who traveled with them each day. They would hire a taxi to take them to the villages and the driver would tell them the history of each town. One such town had a water-delivery stone system that dated back 2000 years. When they left Madrid, Mary Lee bought each of the girls winter coats made from sheep skin. She also bought gifts for all the family and some things for the home.

Mary Lee died in the winter of 1975 while Becky was attending the University of South Carolina, two days before Christmas. It was a terrible time with Becky home from college and Jeannie living in her own apartment at Merrick Place. The Milward Funeral Home took care of the funeral and during the funeral December 26, 1975, the cousins from Lancaster received notice that a double first cousin of Mary Lee's and the cousins father, Chester Engle, had died. Needless to say, that was the family's worst Christmas.

Becky went back to college and Jeannie stayed with her dad for a few weeks.

In the summer of 1976, Walter sold the home at 537 Clinton Road because a realtor came up to him and told him that there was a man and his wife who liked the house and wanted to buy it. Walter told him the price was $150,000 and he would not take a penny less. The buyers came, looked, measured and made a full offer, which Walter accepted. He moved to a rental house located on Moreland Drive. The owner was a university professor who was going away temporarily. The next year, the owner decided to sell and Walter bought the house for the sum of $140,000. It was the former parsonage of the Central Christian Church The house backed to a pond and had a wonderful yard. In the winter months the pond would freeze and the neighbors and children would skate or sleigh ride down the hill onto the pond.

The houses in the area are now selling for over a million dollars.

During his stay at the Moreland Drive Home, Walter had a Christmas dinner for all of his and Mary Lee's relatives, along with Becky and Jeannie. He also held a sale of one of the stores he had purchased from bankruptcy. The basement of the house was unfinished and was a perfect place to hold the sale. Walter had Cinderella cleaning as before and had to travel to downtown every morning to get her and then go to work and the driving was just too much A year later, he decided the upkeep was excessive and again sold the house and moved into another rental unit. His new home was a duplex with a walkout basement in which you entered by a spiral stairway from the upstairs. There was a living room, dining room, two bedrooms, kitchen and family room with a pool table and garage in the basement. The unit was owned by Dudley and Don Webb and after one year, they raised the rent and Walter moved out.

While Walter was away in Florida, he came back and found the back door open and his silver julep cups stolen. Lucky for him, he had put the flatware under the bed and they did not find them. They stole his baby cup and julep cups and a few others. Walter always thought because he had it insured that someone in the insurance business was telling a thief who had silver insured and they targeted the homes for silver, which was at an all-time high of $40 per ounce.

After another year, he bought another small house and moved again. During the time he was in this home in 1978, he had a party for the Seventieth Division reunion officers and friends. He erected a tent in the backyard and had about fifty people to his home. That was the only time the reunion was held in Lexington and was the largest in number ever held by the Seventieth Division Association. The next time he moved was to the town house at 389 South Upper street during the year 1980.

Golf with Walter

Walter played golf at Picadome golf course when he first moved to Lexington and in 1977, the Tates Creek Golf course was charted and Walter was a certificate member.

Walter joined the Lexington Country Club in 1962 after his law partner, His partner, Arthur Rouse, the then president of the club, asked Walter to join. It was a beautiful club and golf course. Walter played golf two or three times each week. During the first years, the club had three or four golf holes along Paris Pike in front of the clubhouse. One member hit a ball across the road leading up to the club and it went through an open window of an auto going up to the clubhouse, hitting the driver. The lady lost the use of one eye because of the golf ball. After the club settled that case, the members bought land in the rear of the golf course, along the railroad tracks. The course was then laid out so all the golf was played behind the clubhouse and the holes in front were closed.

Walter played golf on Wednesdays, Saturdays and Sundays with all his friends. They enjoyed the outings and it was a round-the-year affair, as they played winter golf sometimes in the snow. Walter recalls sweeping snow off some greens so putts could be made. Records were kept regarding the number of birdies, eagles and pars that were made by the winter members and at the end of the season, prizes were awarded at a dinner. There were many dances attended by Mary Lee and Walter, especially on Derby Day, where the shipboard-type racing was enjoyed by all. One Derby Day, a new bartender was making mint juleps and pouring bourbon over crushed ice until he filled the glass with sugar and lime, concealing the taste of bourbon. Many women and some men drank two or three and passed out on couches and chairs in the main part of the club and out on the patio. It was a sight to see and needless to say, the bartender was fired.

One time, Walter was playing golf on a Sunday afternoon and when the eighteen holes were finished and arriving at the Pro Shop, he was told there had been an earthquake. It appears that there is a train track running along the back of the golf course and the foursome must have thought a train was going by and did not notice that the ground shook from the earthquake.

The trophy that Walter enjoys showing more than all the others was a golf day at the Idle Hour Country Club and in  competition with the members of his law firm, Fowler, Measle and Bell. All the players were lawyers and all were at least twenty-five years younger than Walter. Bruce Bell, son of Tommy Bell (now Fayette County District Judge); Roger Cowden, Guy Colson; and others were in competition. At the eighteenth hole, Walter made a thirty-foot putt to win with a ninety-one score.

More Golf with Walter and Friends

On one cold January day in 1989, Walter was playing golf with Larry Roberts, a partner in his law firm and Walter hit a 5 iron on number 4 hole. Larry yelled that it went in the hole. Walter ran all the way to the green to see if it was true. Truly, the ball was in the hole and it is recorded in the PGA records that Walter Cox made a hole in one. One day during a Kiwanis tournament at Woodford Country Club, with Dr. Shepard, Mitch Shepard and one other, Walter hit a shot 150 yards on a par four hole and the ball hit on the front of the green and rolled across and back to the hole and dropped in for an eagle. Angel at work?

Recently, about 2009, Walter was playing a course in Scott County, Kentucky, called Longview. Along the road was a par 5 and although it was a two-man best ball, the drive Walter made was in the middle of the fairway. His partner lost his ball, so they played Walter's drive in the fairway. Walter's next ball was in the fairway about sixty yards short and his partner's ball was in a sand trap next to the green. They elected to hit Walter's ball again and lo and behold, Walter put it in the hole for another eagle. Golf is a hobby but also it is a wonderful way to exercise mentally and physically, according to Walter. This year 2011, at the Bull golf course, Walter won a new pair of golf shoes worth $110 and is he proud of them!

One day, in Fort Myers at the Fort Myers Country Club, Rueben Naylor was playing golf with Walter and on one hole, he hit under the ball, which went straight up in the air and Rueben caught it coming down. One day, at the Lexington Country Club, Walter hit in the sand next to the ninth hole on his third shot. The entire foursome was betting and Walter's partner was already over four on a par four, so the opposite team of the foursome was already counting their money. Walter proceeded to the sand trap and when he exploded the ball out of the sand, it went straight into the hole and he made a par that won the match (angel).

Another funny story was at Rivers Edge Golf Course in Fort Myers when Marty Shaw, Nick Collis and Bill Kokorelis (all brothers-in-law of Walter) were playing. Bill hit a ball on number 7 and it hooked in the water. Bill remarked that he would hit a mulligan and again teed the ball and hit it again in the water. He tried again and the ball went in the water. After counting all his tries, it was determined that he had hit eight balls off the tee in the water on the left. One time, the same foursome were playing a par 3 course in Fort Myers beach and Nick Collis hit a ball on a par 3. The ball was going so fast (a skull) that when it hit the flagpole, it spun around several times and dropped one foot from the hole. If he had not hit the flagstick, the ball would have gone thirty yards past the green. Another unusual event occurred when Marty Shaw and Walter were playing a course at Hilton

Head Island, South Carolina. The cart was air-conditioned with a cooler full of ice and a motor pulling air through the ice in a hose hooked to the back of the cart so it could be directed to the face or neck of the occupants of the cart.

Another unusual time was at a Country Club on the bay near Marty Shaw's home. The cart was filled with all kinds of liquor, soft drinks, ice and glasses for the foursome to drink. It was just like the refrigerator in a hotel room where you are inventoried when you enter and billed for the drinks you use while you are in the room or the cart. (What a way to go!)

Walter played with the senior PGA event at the Griffin Gate golf course and at the party before the next day's game, he drew the flamboyant Doug Sanders. Doug was known for the coordinated clothes he wore. He had all different colors of his apparel and shoes to match. It was said that he had 200 pairs of shoes, all different color to choose from. Walter had a green outfit consisting of green pants and shirt, so he bought a green cap and also bought some green paint with which to paint his white golf shoes. The morning of the game, when Doug came up on the tee and saw Walter with his bright green outfit, he remarked, "It appears as if someone had been to a Pittsburg Paint store." Doug was great to play with and he was great with all the girls on the course. He kissed everyone of the ones where he could get close enough while riding in his own cart. On the ninth hole (the hole that runs uphill along side of the hotel and is a par 5), Walter was on the green in four strokes and above the hole. Doug lined him up and told him he could make the putt.

The Lexington Country Club members were working that hole as volunteers and when Walter sunk the putt for a par, the entire group clapped and yelled for Walter.

The first time the senior PGA played the Griffin Gate Course, it had just been completed and was wet and muddy, so the players were allowed to lift, clean and place their balls. Arnold Palmer was playing with Walter and his group and he explained the rule to them.

"When you are allowed to move the ball, you must place it with your hand because if you roll it with your club, as all of us do, it is considered a stroke every time the club touches the ball." Walter and Pam had their picture made with Arnold that night at the Marriott (see picture).

Once when Walter was playing Charles Jett Jr., who was a client and friend (president of the Bank of the Bluegrass), he won $10 from Charley. A twenty-dollar bill was produced by Charley, who proceeded to tear the bill in half. He presented the half of the twenty to Walter and told him he would have to win the other half in order to spend it.

A friend of Walters, Bud Beattie and he were playing the nine-hole course on Captiva Island at the Plantation. Bud was an engineer with IBM and was instrumental in inventing the ball typewriter, which was introduced in 1955, along with some 1200 hundred other patents. On the third hole, a par 3, Bud hit the 160-yard shot and it went in the hole for a hole in one. Needless to say, Bud was elated and never forgot that great day when he and Walter played Captiva.

One time in 1986, Pam and Walter were visiting Miami at Marty Shaw and Elpita's home. Walter volunteered to serve as a marshal for the Senior PGA at the Key Biscayne golf course. While doing so, Walter walked along with Arnold Palmer's caddie. He asked the caddie if he also played golf. The caddie replied that he was busy with Arnold 364 days of each year, as Arnold either played or practiced every day except Christmas.

Another interesting day of golf was at Keys Gate golf course at Homestead Florida. The foursome in front of Walter, Marty, Bill and George were slow because one of the foursome was wading out in the water, getting his ball. It seems there were many balls in the water and as a result of the guy being in the water, he just started collecting golf balls and throwing them on the fairway. There must have been twenty-five or more golf balls thrown out of the water before Walter and his group started yelling at the guy. He apologized and went to collect his balls and continue playing. Of course, that is no different than Marty collecting balls every afternoon at Rivers Edge Golf Course (now Gulf Harbor) at Fort Myers, Florida. Marty would come in every afternoon with ten or more balls, but this one time, he stayed and stayed and when he finally came to the house after dark, he had golf balls in every pocket in his shirt, all the way around and it was determined that he had picked up sixty-three balls. It seems he too went into the water and collected balls from all those errant hitters.

One occasion, while Marty Shaw was visiting Lexington, Walter and Dick Naylor took him to Prestonburg, Ky to play golf where there is a swnging bridge across the river. The first hole is straight up the mountain and is only 125 yards but it is hard to reach with a driver. Another hole runs parallel with another hole and it seems as if you are hitting the balls at the players on the oncoming hole. It is probably the most interesting course in Kentucky.

Return to the Battle Fields

In 1977, Walter was informed that the 70th Infantry Division Association members were going to Germany to retrace their steps.

There were 75 wives and husbands who signed up for the trip.

The trip departed from New York and was on an India Airlines 747 plane. The plane was delayed until about 2:00 A. M.

Most of the group in the association went to sleep soon after takeoff but Walter decided to see if the India stewardesses dressed in sarongs could take him up to the upper lounge which was located just behind the pilots. They told him he; was lucky because there was not a single person booked for that area. The girls took him to the lounge, fixed him a drink of scotch, introduced him to the pilots who showed him the instruments and everything in the cockpit. After he had enough of looking around, the nice little ladies informed him the could sleep up there in a long retractable lounge chair. It turned out to be the best flight he had ever experienced.

After arriving in Frankfurt, Germany two buses were ready to board and the group were on their merry way. Walters army and University of Kentucky friend was on the same bus with his wife, Paul and Walter decided to take over the loud speaker in order to ask everyone to tell what they did during War II. The wives told some great stories about working in factories making war materials, going to high school, college and other interesting facts. It was a great way to break the ice and make everyone familiar with each other. The men told where the were in the Division and where they fought the war. The first stop was SAARBRUCKEN the city where we crossed the Saar river into Germany. The city was rebuilt and the Hotel was plush. The following day, the buses took the group to the towns of Wingen and Bushweiller where the 70th Division first landed and fought. The city of Wingen, welcomed the men and showed them the new modern city. The Church was not touched during the war but it had been improved over the past 32 years and of course, was the center of attention. This was the church where Cox and his platoon relieved the 250 prisoners on January 6, 1945. From that area the next stop was Forbach and Sterling Wendell. The City mayor and other business men welcomed everyone and took them to City Hall where pictures were posted of the City as it looked immediately after being shot up during the shelling. It was a real experience and they also had wine tasting to make it even more enjoyable. To top it off, the returnees were taken to a restaurant where the meal was one to top all others. First came the wine, beer, cognac and tidbits so delectable that it was too good to be true. Then came the meal with none other than piglets (one for each plate) apparently unborn. The meat was so tender, that it just melted in your mouth. More and more came with courses of food of all kinds together with the booze. About 3:00 in the afternoon, Paul Durbin, Fran

Wilis and Walter tried to sing "MY OLD KENTUCKY HOME" It was really bad because they were half drunk, slurring the words which they could not remember and just ad libbed. Fran Willis was the wife of Colonel Willis and were newly weds December 7, 1941. She was from Kentucky and a registered nurse and he was a recent graduate from the West Point academy.

After the wonderful lunch, dinner, the townspeople took the group up into the hills overlooking Forbach. There in the middle of the newly grown trees, Walter found a fox hole the men had dug in 1945 preparation for invading the City. The hole was filled in with leaves and one side was partially caved in, but it was evident that it was the one Walter had occupied. The trees were so large one could hardly see the town as compared to 1945 when they were bare and Walter had good observation. He had the flashback of being there and seeing the town burning, bombs hitting the houses, an observation plane flying and dodging around over the town, just as one would see in a war movie. The scene was one he could not forget and it gave him goose bumps and fear. He also thought about the possibility of stepping a mine that remained on the battlefield so he was glad to get off the mountain and back into town safe and sound.

From there the next stop was along the Rhine river where the group were billeted in houses overlooking the river. There was room for 6 in each house and they were authenic giving the men a touch of the past. They were farm houses that had the lower level for the animals so the smell permeated the entire house. It was not pleasant and they were glad to be away the next day.

The SS troops that had been the enemy in Wingen, were having a reunion in BOMBACH. The 70th men were invited to attend one of their meetings and the invitation was accepted. Walter was really intimidated when the groups met. The Germans were not in uniform but in agrarian clothes which resembled uniforms and Walter thought what if they pulled out their pistols and shot us at this late date. They were all speaking German and were not understood but some interpreters helped so there was some conversation between everyone.

Walter 3rd from left in Germany

The meeting was successful as 26 of them came to the 70th assn. in St Louis the very next year 1978. One of the men was a lawyer who took Walter in his Mercedes to see the Villa where Walter's Company were billeted after the War. The place was locked up and could not be entered but was a highlight of the trip. The lawyer was a coal company lawyer and spoke English. He told

Walter-German-Paul Durbin

about being young and thinking that Germany was saving the world. He told about being brainwashed at age 14 and of course, later learned how terrible the Germans were.

Later, he visited Walter in Lexington and has invited him to visit his home in Germany but Walter has never been back on any of the return trips the Division Association makes each year.

Lt George Blanchard who was B Company commander when Walter was E Company Commander, was now Major General in charge of all of the American tropps in Germany. He arranged for the Army Band to play for the German SS association and the 70th asso to pay tribute to the Americans and Germans killed in the War II. He was criticized in many articles later for celebrating the German soldiers.

The trip ended as the first trip back to the battlegrounds of the 70th Infantry Division but has continued every year since then and will go again in 2013.

New Abode Downtown

In 1980, Darrell Hancock, T. J. Moses and Walter bought a lot at the corner of Maxwell and Upper and proceeded to hire a wrecking company to tear down the burned-out hulk of a building. The historical committee found out and obtained a court order to stop tearing the building down until a hearing was obtained before the committee to determine if the building had significant historical content. It took two months to have the hearing and get approval. Before Walter bought the lot, vagrants were sleeping in the building and setting fires to heat their food and it was a sore spot for the neighborhood. So the committee finally was convinced that there was no historical value to the building and allowed the old building to be torn down.

Walter & Dad

The three condos were finally constructed and Walter had the corner spot with a two-car garage in the lower level, along with the laundry and a recreation room, which contained a bar and ping-pong table. The second floor consisted of a living room, great room that contained a kitchen, bar,

Pic of Walter and Senator McConnell of Kentucky.

pool table, dining area and a half bath. The third floor contained two large bedrooms and two baths and the master bedroom sported a Jacuzzi. This Jacuzzi created a lot of fun and it seemed that the feminine visitors always wanted to know how to get in the tub. There were mirrors surrounding the tub on two walls and a small lamp that gave off a nice glow for those in the tub. The one time it was used in an unusual way was when Pam's sister was getting married and Walter had a bachelor party for her prospective husband. One of the dancing girls was in attendance and she was in the tub with a lot of the guys including Walter. Whew!

The condo was the subject of a lot of fund-raisers for Republicans especially one for and other charities and fun times with a lot of parties. (Picture above of Mitch McConnell's first run for the Senate in Walters condo in Lexington 1984)

Walter would walk home at noon each day and eat leftovers and take a nap while sitting at the kitchen table. The rear of the building could be entered by way of a spiral stair that led to a runway servicing all three condos. There was a courtyard out back for the auto entrance and an iron gate that operated automatically. Walter decorated an artificial Christmas tree the first year and, from then on, kept it in a closet in the lower floor and just retrieved it every Christmas for decoration. He also read a book about "The Girl in the Red Velvet Swing" and decided when the building was under construction to hang a swing in his large master bedroom. There was a steel beam holding the roof just in the middle of the bedroom, so Walter had the builder drill two holes in the steel beam with which to attach the swing. When they plastered the ceiling, the hooks were exposed for the ropes of the swing. Walter built a seat and had it padded with red velvet to be attached to the ropes. This swing created a sensation in Lexington and everyone wanted to see the red velvet swing. It really was used by the kids who came to visit more than any of the girls everyone thought used it.

There was a cleaning lady who came every Monday and Friday. Her name was Cinderella (really) and everyone had a hard time believing that was her real name. She did the cleanup and laundry and sometimes cooked for the entertainment. If there was a party, Walter would have Cindy cook and put out the food for the invitees and then stay and cleanup afterward. One particular time after a convention in New Orleans, which was for the Commercial Law League of America, he brought home or had shipped a box full of oysters. All of his friends were called and a night of oysters on the half shell were served raw. This was a day to remember. Many times after a dove shoot, Cinderella would prepare the doves for all the men and also prepare chicken for the ladies. Very few ladies would eat the dove, but they would eat the chicken.

While Walter was in Kiwanis on a Tuesday, his friend Dr. Sam Warren, talked about a small house he owned off Third Street here in Lexington. It seems that Sam wanted to sell the house and carry the mortgage. Walter told Dr. Sam that he would buy it and pay the $7,000 on a monthly basis based on a fifteen-year payout at 5 percent interest. Sam went for it and Walter let Cinderella have the mortgage and house. She paid the $40 every month for the entire fifteen years and when she died, the home sold for $30,000.

Trips for Hunting

During 1983, Walter, Jack Banahan and Billy Forbess flew in Billy's plane to Canada to go bear hunting. Billy's family had a lodge there in an area 200 miles north of Toronto. The trip was to Cleveland and then to the Lake in Canada, where they were met by the family and transported to the camp. They arrived about 1:00 p.m. and by 4:00 p.m. were out in a bear stand up in a tree. The stand consisted of a board nailed to a limb with some more boards to climb up to the stand. Walter sat there with his legs hanging off the seat from 4:00 p.m. until 8:00 p.m. and saw nothing. He was thinking that he was silly for going to Canada in the first place and to go bear hunting all by himself in a tree in this godforsaken place was so bizarre that he started to get down. About the time he made that decision, he looked up and a bear came out of the woods about seventy-five feet in front of him. The bear had its back to the stand and Walter carefully brought his 30-30 Winchester rifle up to his shoulder and about that time, the bear whirled and looked up and took off. One shot from that rifle was enough to down the bear and as it turned out, it was exactly in the bear's heart. Walter stayed in the tree for a long time and finally was convinced that the bear was dead, so he climbed down and went to the road for help. A truck with two men came by and were glad to drive their truck to retrieve the bear and take Walter to camp. The same thing happened to Billy Forbess, as he also killed a bear the same afternoon, except that Bill's bear did not die immediately but had to be tracked for a few hundred yards. It seemed also that Bill was not put in a tree but in an abandoned car hull to wait for his bear.

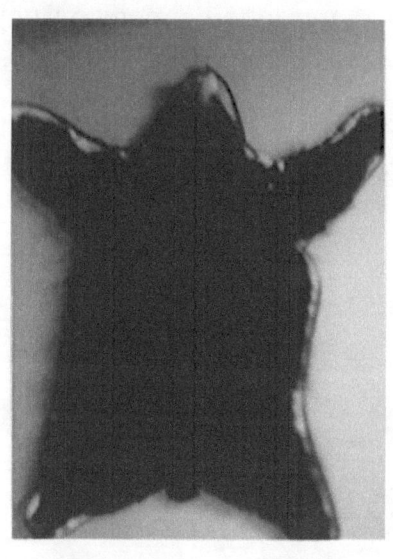

The fellows at the camp, stripped the bear skin and the meat. The skin was saved and Walter has it in his basement hanging on a wall. The meat was frozen and carried by plane back home, where a bear feast was arranged and surprise, everyone enjoyed the meat. Cinderella prepared it as a roast and it tasted somewhat like a pig roast. He had chicken for the people (ladies) who would not eat the bear meat, but to his surprise, the ladies also ate the bear meat. Since one bear was all you could have, the three of them went fishing on a lake close to the cabin. The fish were special to the area in Canada, weighing about two to three pounds and were a special delicacy for the region. Walter learned to eat the eyes of the fish, which were considered the best part of the fresh fish there on the Canadian lake.

Another time, maybe in 1977, Walter, Dick Naylor and T. J. Moses all drove in Walter's station wagon to Mississippi to hunt dove with Dick's cousin. They started the trip about 11:00 p. m. and by 3:00 were in Tennessee at a Civil War cemetery. Walter drove for two hours and then laid down in the back and went to sleep. As the group drove into the cemetery Walter woke up when the car stopped. Walter was looking at nothing but headstones and immediately thought he was dead and gone to a place of repose. They laughed a lot about the reaction to the tombstones. They drove all night and finally arrived and found a motel, went to bed and got five hours of sleep before the dove shoot. They entered the field at 3:00 p.m. and doves were flying everywhere. Before 5:00 p.m., almost everyone had killed so many doves that they had run out of shotgun shells.

Walter   TJ Moses   Dick Naylor

Walter with pheasant

The birds were piled up in a stack about two feet high (picture) and Walter asked how we are going to clean them. They were told that they had enough locals to take care of all the dove; therefore, the shooters could go home, have a drink and eat steak. The next day, the same thing took place and more shells were purchased for the additional dove that had escaped the day before. Another pile of dove (picture) was produced and again the cleaning was left up to the African American neighbors.

The cousins announced another possibility of bird hunting, that being quail. It seems that the farm had a provision for raising quail and then turn them loose in the fields so they could be hunted and shot at. They had three dogs to find the birds, point them and allow the group to shoot. The hunting was done along fence rows and where there was cover for the quail to hide. While Walter was walking down one field, he looked out in front and there was a wildcat up in a tree. It was 200 yards away, but the buckshot from the shotgun caused the cat to scamper down and run for his life. It was a beautiful sight to see and the first one Walter had ever witnessed. After three or four hours of quail hunting, the bags were filled again with birds and the shooting stopped. Another day of bliss had taken place for this Kentucky group visiting Mississippi. One other thing took place that was unusual, that being picking up pecans from all the pecan trees growing wild in this farm country. Each one filled a large brown sack full of pecans and Walter took his home and all winter long, ate pecans from Mississippi, a successful hunting trip provided by Dick Naylor and his cousins from a Southern state.

Fishing Trips

Along about that year or the year after that, Charley Lear, a friend and local insurance executive; Charley's son; and Walter drove to Nova Scotia on a fishing trip. They caught a ferry in Maine to go to Halifax. It had been a long drive, so Walter rented a bed and slept for the six-hour boat ride. Charlie and his son gambled at the slot machines and blackjack. The auto went with them on the trip, so when they arrived on shore, it was a drive up to the little village of Ecumsecum, where they rented a cottage to stay while fishing. Nova Scotia reminded Walter of Kentucky in the 1930s. Women hung their clothes on lines, country stores had sugar and flour in barrels, the clothes were overalls and gingham dresses and life was slow.

They contacted a boat owner who fished for large tuna in the Bay of Funde and out in the ocean, about six miles where the reef drops off to six miles deep. They fished for two days, sitting on the fan tail in a seat with a large fishing pole and dragging behind it about ten mackerel as bait. The boat was about forty feet and had sleeping quarters, a kitchen and bathroom. Being unlucky, no fish was caught, so regular fishing then took place and very deep. Several types of fish were caught that were strange-looking but, according to the captain, were good to eat. He prepared the fish immediately on the boat and there never could be better-tasting fish than prepared like that. Later on, after the boat returned and found the Bay about 100 feet higher in tide than it was in the morning when the boat left, which is one of the places in the world that the tide is that abnormal. It is the Bay of Fundi, visited by all who go to Nova Scotia.

The three visited a country store and met some men there who told of having tuna in a net out in the ocean. They explained that the net was a trap where small tuna came in through a small opening and then could not escape. The men then would feed the large tuna until they weighed 600 or 700 pounds and then sell them to the Japanese for $4 per pound.

It sounded so intriguing that they went with the boat to catch the mackerel and feed them to the tuna. The boat was thirty feet long and had an auto motor for traveling fast. On arriving at the fishing spot, some fish were thrown out to chum the other mackerel fish. When the men were ready, they handed Walter and Charles fishing lines with five or seven hooks on the line and red cloth attached to each hook. The lines were dropped into the ocean and almost immediately, all hooks would be engaged by a fish weighing two to 3 pounds. The line would be thrown into the bottom of the boat and the fish would wiggle loose. The line would be thrown in again and the procedure repeated. After about thirty or forty minutes, the boat was filled with these mackerel and Walter asked if they were going to swamp the boat as it was dangerously loaded to within four inches above the water. Now the boat was carefully negotiated over the net and into the center of it. The fish were thrown into the water and out came the big tuna. For the next thirty minutes, all of them were throwing the fish into the air and the tuna were leaping into the air to catch them. It was a show like you would never see in your lifetime. It was better than a dolphin show in Miami or Orlando. Pictures were taken and it was hard to convince friends back home that this episode really took place. The men who had the fish told Walter that they would sell the tuna to the Japanese in the spring for $4 per pound and they estimated they had six fish weighing over 3,500 pounds. That trip to Nova Scotia was a once-in-a-lifetime for Walter. Recently Walter read that the big tuna were now selling for $200.00 per pound with the Japanese being the buyers.

One trip to Captiva, while being a scavenger on the beach for shells, Walter came up to the end of Captiva and there were thousands of horseshoe crabs on the sand mating. It was a sight to see, so thick that you could not step without stepping on one of them. One such person they met on the beach was a bearded man who looked like a vagabond with a long white beard but was really a retired Coca-Cola executive. He had built a boat that was over 100 feet long. The yacht looked as if it were a miniature ship. He had sold his home and moved all of his expensive paintings, silver and china. He could travel by ocean for 700 miles on one tank of diesel. Walter had never witnessed anything like it and talked about it for years. The man invited the entire family to come aboard to see the hand-built yacht.

In 1967, Charlie Jett talked about lending money to Walter to buy a home with a swimming pool that was for sale on the bay for only $34,000, but at the time, daughter Jeannie was in college and money was tight, so that idea was given up. After visiting the island for each year thereafter, Walter finally bought a lot on the island for only $7,000 and teamed up with a builder from Lexington and Peter Perlman, a lawyer in his office, to build a home. The builder built the 1,800-square-foot, three-bed, two-bath one-story home for the total sum of $40,000. It was sold in 1975 because it was impossible to keep up since all three owned the house together and Walter was the only one footing the bills. Walter then bought a villa on the gulf, from the South Seas Plantation for $75,000 and devised a time-sharing contract with nine others, most of them friends and fellow attorneys. Darrell Hancock and Walter drew up the contract, which was a very detailed contract where each shareholder shared five weeks per year. Two weeks in the fall, two weeks in the winter or spring and one week in the summer. It cost $7,500 each and each had to share the yearly expenses. At a meeting held each year, a drawing was held to determine what series of time sharing the shareholders would have for the forthcoming year. It was the first (time share) that he had heard about, but it is still working, although Walter sold out his interest.

Thereafter, he and T. J. Moses bought two tennis villas and one bay villa from the South Seas Plantation and sold them before they were a month old. T. J. Moses and his wife, Ginger, accompanied Walter on a trip to furnish the two tennis villas and were there on the island when the large restaurant opened. It was a grand opening, with the Governor of Florida, representatives and stock holders of the South Seas Plantation being present. Ginger, T. J. and Walter had worked on the condo all day and were in T-shirts when they attended the gala function because they did not realize that it was a dress-up affair. Many of the people who attended were wearing evening dresses and tuxedos. During the party, they had a bar in every part of this restaurant and Walter ordered a drink at each one of them. They had to sleep on the mattresses delivered during the day but on the floor since the beds would arrive the next day.

Walter and T. J. went to a furniture store in Fort Myers to buy enough furniture to furnish the two condos. They picked out all the necessities and told the owner that they wanted two just alike. He gave them a price of $6,000, but T. J. said to the owner that they would only pay $4,000. The owner said no, but when T. J. started putting cash on the table in twenties, the owner grabbed the money before T. J. could scoop it up and leave. It was evident that the cash talked. The furniture was delivered to the condos and only the mattress was delivered so Walter had to sleep on the floor on the mattress that night. Walter and T. J. sold the tennis villas for a nice profit.

The beach cottage was a great place to take his friends to play golf and many times four, five, or six would go for a week to play golf and enjoy the amenities of the island of Captiva. One such vacation was with Jeannie, Becky, Frances Engle Brooking and Glen's widow, Elizabeth Gulley Cox. They all ate together each night and scoured the beaches during the day. It was 1976, just the summer after Mary Lee died.

Walter's father, Walter Clay Cox Sr., was stricken with diabetes when he was forty-nine. He went from being a man weighing 180 pounds down to 125 pounds. Being a stubborn man, Senior refused to go to the doctor even though he knew that he had diabetes. One day, Walter told Dad that he was going to go to Dr. Edwards's office and that if he refused, he would pick him up and carry him to the office. Senior agreed finally and was examined by Dr. Edwards and was put on insulin, which he used to balance his life. He gave himself a shot of insulin every day until the day he died at age eighty-four. When the funeral for his dad was held, Walter put cigars in his dads coat pocket and a racing form under his arm. He also had a student at the school play (*Call to the Post*) on a trumpet, as his father always loved and bet on the horses. Walter's father left a will giving one half to him and one half to Glen's daughter, Peggy Lou. There was a farm with 119 acres on Dix river that Walter bought from the estate and thereafter sold to Dan Trinler who built a home and barn and resides there now.

Becky & Walter

Newly Married

Walter was the office manager of the law firm Fowler, Measle and Bell, for a period of the last eight years of his practice, from 1980 to 1988. There were between fifteen and eighteen attorneys associated with the firm, but the partners totaled only seven. An administrator was hired to manage the firm. She was with the firm for a couple of years when one Christmas at the firm party, she brought her sister, Pam Collis, to the party. When Walter met Pam, it was love at first sight because he took her to his office, closed the door and kissed her. He announced that this is the girl I am going to marry. They took three years to finally take the step to marry, but it was predestined to happen when they met.

She was a lady filled with laughter, beautiful beyond words, dark-haired, petite and just a joy to be with. Walter spent much time every night at her home into the wee hours, sometime sleeping on the couch before the TV. Her father had previously been stricken with a stroke that affected his speech; however, it was obvious he liked Walter.

If Walter did not come to visit the family or take Pam out, he would ask where is Walter? In 1983 when President, George H. W. Bush was Inaugurated He and Pam were invited to go so they visited Becky in Washington, D. C. at her apartment. It was a highlight of a lifetime and the dance was fantastic.

Pam and Walter traveled to San Francisco, where they visited the Redwood Forests, to Puerto Rico and made a trip around the island; they went to New Mexico and there they visited the Indian reservation. In the winter of 1987 while Walter was practicing law and Pam was in Miami, Walter phoned Pam and proposed marriage. She told him to get down on his knees and take a picture and he did.

She accepted and within a week she had returned to Lexington. At Easter 1988, Bill Kokorelis and Maria (Pam's sister) invited everyone in the family to come to Connectcut for a party to celebrate the engagement of Walter and Pam. It was a great get together with the men playing golf, the women cooking and the kids playing in the backyard. Bill prepared and roasted a Lamb, they all attended church every night during the Easter week and a ceremony took place on Easter making the engagement final. The two married July 3, 1988, at the Greek Orthodox Church in Lexington.

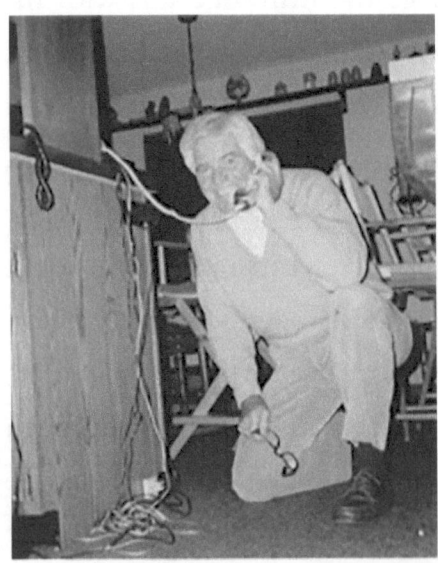
Walter proposing

The church was filled with friends and overflowing into the basement and outside. Dick Naylor, Walter's best friend, was second best man and Andy Tsiboukas, who was a friend of the Collis family, served as best man.

Dick Naylor & Walter

Tom Wakefield - Jeannie - Walter Pam Becky & Kip Wood

picture on steps of church of attendees who were relatives.

Walter's daughters Jeannie and Tom and Becky and Kip were in attendance, along with many other members of his family.

Pam arranged a great reception at a local hotel with about 200 people for dinner. The reception was one to remember with introductions of all of the guests, dancing by everyone, speeches by anyone wanting to talk, glasses tinkling so Pam and Walter could KISS. At 12:00 Walter ask Pam to leave to go to their room at another Hotel. She said she was staying to dance some more. At 2:00 Walter again ask her to leave and she replied "You can go but I am staying" They finally left about 3:00 A. M. Their only problem was with the family of a sister, Elpitha Shaw, from Miami. A stomach virus hit Martin Shaw, Elpitha's husband, one of the groomsmen and he had to leave the church while the ceremony was being conducted. Others in the family, including Martin Shaw IV (age two), came down with the same stomach virus.

One particular guest at the wedding was an ex-soldier in Walter's E Company. Tom Dickinson was a scout in the platoon and thereafter became the head librarian at the New York Central Library. Tom sported a beard and looked older than Walter, so when introductions took place, he was introduced as Walter's commanding general. This is the first time this story has been told. The next morning about 11:00 Walter and Pam went to Pam's home where everyone from out of town were gathered. Before they could walk into the house, there was a particular ceremony about life and some food was served to them on the steps. Another celebration for 2 hours and then Walter and Pam left for a honeymoon. Pam had no idea where she was going but the Plane left for Atlanta and then on to Seattle Washington.

Incidentally, the honeymoon was on Whidbey Island, near Seattle, Washington. The only access to the island was by ferry, so after arriving by plane, a car was rented and Walter and Pam, (Mr. and Ms. Walter C. Cox Jr.), drove to the ferry and were taken to the island.

The bed and breakfast house that was an A-frame was a real delight. It was located on the ocean high above the water. The entire side of the building was glass looking out at the ocean. It was two stories, with the dining room and living room with a fireplace on the first floor and two bedrooms on the second floor. There were stereo systems throughout and when morning came, the owners, who resided in an apartment over the garage, would ring a bell and breakfast was served on china and crystal. There was a hot tub outside overlooking the sea and a step system down to the ocean. What a place for a honeymoon. They carried a large five-pound pebble from the beach to their home and it still has a place near the garage. Pam got sick like Marty and for a couple of days, it was touch and go about her stomach virus.

After three days, Walter and Pam again drove to the ferry and debarked where they spent three more days exploring that beautiful island. There were flowers everywhere and one special garden, Burchard Gardens, that no one could ever forget. There was an old car museum, a railroad museum and many other exciting things to do. Pam finally got over the virus only to be followed by Walter having to upchuck like everyone else had. Even though they were briefly sick, they had a grand time and would never forget that honeymoon. The trip had been recommended by the president of the Citizens Union Bank, who was a golfer whom Walter played golf with. He told Walter he was so convinced that Pam would love it that if she did not like it, he would pay for their trip. The marriage was really like *The Big Fat Greek Wedding* movie. Fun fun fun. Pam was and is the angel sent to him and love is the theme of this marriage. Walter cannot believe his good luck that came when he married Pam.

1980 New Home in Ft Myers

After that, the golf course on Captiva became too expensive and crowded, so Walter sold his interest in the condo located on Captiva. He then built a small two-bedroom two-bathroom house on Rivers Edge Golf Course. From 1980 until 1988, he would go to the home as often as he could and play golf with many of his Lexington, Kentucky, friends. This was before Pam and Walter were married. After they married in 1988, they spent a lot of time from January to April there in Fort Myers, together with Pam's sisters, Elpitha and Alkimini, who lived in Miami. They had some good parties for Walters golfing friends and also had good times looking for golf balls.

Elpitha's husband, Marty, loved to look for balls and his pastime after a golf game was to go fill his pockets with golf balls. Every January or February, Walter invited three of his Lexington Country Club friends or some others and they would spend a week playing golf at Fort Myers with all the Lexington group who played golf once each week at some course. Walter's daughters, Becky and husband Kip and Jeannie and husband Tom, visited the vacation home many times. Jeannie would leave daughter, Katherine, age three or four for a week while she and Tom would visit a reserve somewhere on the East Coast. Walter and Pam would take her to the pool, play miniature golf and many other fun times. Becky visited with Sarah and enjoyed the warmth of Florida.

Katherine - Walter's granddaughter

After Walter contracted for the house, other golfing friends also bought nearby. Joe Tuttle and his wife, Wilda; Jack Banahan and his wife; Jeannie and Tom Wakefield and his father, Morry; George Ruschell and wife, Ms. Begley; and Jack Taylor and his daughter, Norma. Over the years, the River's Edge area was renamed Gulf Harbor and became a plush place with million-dollar houses and condos with a large boat dock protected from the gulf.

The house that Walter built, where he had so much enjoyment in, was on the outskirts of this new area and looked as if the servants of the rich and famous lived there. The twelve or thirteen years that Walter and Pam visited the River's Edge Subdivision and golf course were filled with friends, relatives and fun. Many parties were held there and many of the days, Walter played golf and Pam either worked on the house, painting, decorating and washing and ironing or sitting by the heated pool. They had a paradise in Florida and enjoyed each and every day they stayed at the house. Most of the time, they stayed from January until April and then came back to Lexington, where they lived at the townhouse at 389 South Upper Street. Many times, they would go over to Miami and stay with Pam's sisters, Elpitha and Alkimini and their husbands.

After returning to Lexington, Walter played golf at the Lexington Country Club, where he had been a member and vice president. They would attend the dances, eat Sunday lunch, go to the bingo games and sometimes Pam would play golf for nine holes. One day, when she was playing the third hole which was a very long par 4 even for the girls, she hit a shot that struck a robin and killed it. So Walter told the guys at the club that Pam got a birdie on the fourth hole and they were shocked. Of course, the real story was finally related and it was the subject of much discussion.

During Easter of 1994, after staying all winter in Miami, Pam and Walter took a vacation to Palm Springs, California, by flying to San Diego and renting an automobile to drive up to Palm Springs. The flowers were in bloom and the trip was absolutely fabulous. There were windmills all over the hillsides turning in the breeze, there were wildflowers and the hills were alive with unusual things. Pam stopped and cut the wildflowers to bring home for her garden. The year was 1994 and the month was April. The condo was nice, the city was beautiful with lush grass and flowers and sand and the desert was just across the road. It was an oasis in the middle of the desert. They visited the Indian Reservation, where the Indians had large homes because the land all belonged to them and they lease it to the City of Palm Springs and the occupants of the land receiving large sums of money to live royally. Bob Hope's 30,000-square-foot home up in the hills was a sight to see as were the date trees and golf courses. They searched for a Greek Orthodox Church to attend Easter services and finally found it after many trips up and down the roads. It was a small ex-school and the services were held outside.

The people were friendly and welcomed Walter and Pam. The trip ended in San Diego and a few special places were visited there in the old part of town.

The special event that occurred later was the birth of their son, Walter Clay Cox III, on January 23, 1995, which just happened to be nine months after the vacation in California. (His Angel worked overtime.) Pam and Walter went to the University of

Kentucky Hospital at 7:30 a.m. on January 25, 1985 and Walter watched as the delivery took place. The doctor wrapped the baby in a sheet and handed him to Walter with instructions to take him next door to the nurse who would clean him. A video tape was recording all this and from the looks of the way the nurse who went about her business, Walter thought she would kill the baby, Clay, as he is called. He was a perfect specimen and still is. He became the center of everything and after living in the townhouse on the streets of downtown Lexington, Pam and Walter decided that they must move to the outskirts, where Clay would have room to play and grow. In the Fall of 1995, they contracted to build a home in the finest subdivision in Lexington and all of Kentucky, namely, Hartland.

WHAT? A BOY

They chose a corner lot and started the construction of a two-story home. The weather caused the delay of the construction until September 1996, at which time the family moved into Hartland. In the meantime, they sold the townhouse and moved nearby in a rental home so they could oversee the everyday building of their home. They were in the rental home for almost one year during the time of Clay's first birthday. Clay slept in a bed on the first floor, along with Walter and Pam. He was a good boy and slept all night without disturbing the family.

Once when Walter and Pam were eating at the Lexington Country Club, Pam ate a lot of chickpeas. During the night she was feeling bad and she and Walter went to the emergency room at the University of Kentucky Medical Center. After waiting for two or three hours, she was examined and told to go home. The next day, Dr. Peter Sawaya, a special friend who lives on Hartland Parkway and attends the Greek Orthodox Church, looked at the results of the examination done the night before and came to their house and took Pam to the hospital. She had gall stones and were inflamed to the point that Peter was really worried. After obtaining the best doctor at UK, Pam was put on antibiotics for a day or so before the operation. During that time, since Pam was breast-feeding Clay, Walter had to take him to the hospital for his feeding. At night, the only way Walter could get Clay to go to sleep was to put him in the car seat and drive around until he went to sleep and then carry him to bed. Pam recovered and was home in four days, but she really gave everyone a scare regarding the gall stones. After the operation, Pam recovered quickly, as she is the picture of health and maintains her beauty and weight throughout the marriage.

One trip Walter and Pam made was to Puerto Rico. After leaving the airport, they rented an auto and proceeded to drive around the island. The first encounter of uncontrolled traffic was a stop light where every car wanted to go at the same time. They ignored the stop light and all jammed together under the light. One at a time, for an hour or more, the cars would move slowly and weave in and out and finally emerge out of the intersection. They drove across the island to the south and came upon the ocean, where many fishing vessels were located at the dock. They stopped at a motel and toured the dock. A sign proclaiming a trip on a boat the next morning, featuring scuba diving, lunch and sightseeing. They signed up for the trip and, the next morning, appeared at the dock ready to go. Not another person appeared and when the captain announced he was ready to start, Walter told him it was OK if he did not want to go without more people. The captain firmly told Walter that he was going to take the two of them on the trip. The vessel was old and red in color but was seaworthy and fun. They sailed out into the ocean and finally stopped for scuba diving. Then at lunch, the captain cooked a fish lunch with wine and laughed about the lack of persons to entertain. It turned out to be a delightful little trip. After that, they drove around the rest of the island and visited various historic places on the island.

Another four-day weekend was when the two flew to Albuquerque, New Mexico. They were having a festival with a display of Indian wares and handmade objects, but the mountaintop at the Indian Reservation was the most interesting. It appears that there are large areas that rise up out of the normal landscape, which appeared to be 150 feet high and with no way to get to the top, as they are straight up all around the area. However, the Indians have dug a pathway to the top and of course, Walter and Pam decided to see the top of this unusual oddity. Some Indians still live there and have their church and school high on this odd place. One of the most unusual parts were the outdoor privies. They were so located that they hung over the steep walls so that when used, the debris would fall down the sides of the steep area. It worked but it was unforgettable. At one point, there were steps down the steep hill and holes in the wall. Pam threw pebbles toward the hole and they went in, which indicated in Indian lore that she would give birth to a son.

During that period of time, Walter was in the position "of counsel" with his old law firm and went to the firm most every day. He had a few clients to take care of and gave them to other lawyers in the firm to represent and received 25 percent of the fee without doing anything for the client himself. For the fall and winter, they drove to Miami and spent time with Pam's sisters,

Alkimini and Elpitha. Walter played golf with Pam's brothers-in-law, Martin L. Shaw III, Ted Gregor and others.

After the home at 4830 Wyndhurst was finished and they moved in about November 1996, with no sod on the bare ground around the house. They just left the home and went to Florida for the winter and came back in March of 1997, when they undertook to finish the landscaping of the home. The top soil on the bare ground had been washed away down the street and gathered in front of the neighbor's (Tom and Loraye Jones) house. Tom asked Walter if they could not do something about it and Walter immediately called the builder and had sod put down and the street cleaned.

The landscaping was strictly laying sod on the dirt and Walter and Pam individually took upon themselves to plant shrubs and trees. All of this was done over the following year and lo and behold, it was less costly at $900 compared to the $3,000 quoted from a nursery and very well done, so that now the final touch looks fantastic. Pam even built rock walls and gardens in the rear and side of the lot. The stones were gathered from places where the limestone was being overturned by new interstate roads and new construction sites. Walter and Pam hauled the stones in their Van a few at a time, eventually making nice walls. A friend brought dirt from the Kentucky River to fill in behind the rock walls. Pam and her sisters made curtains and drapes and Pam painted the entire home while taking care of her mother. Walter could not and still does not believe she could do all of it, but she did and it is fabulous.

After they moved in to the new home and Walter was babysitting or keeping Clay, when he was about a year old, Walter put Clay on the kitchen counter and before he could be caught, he fell off backward and hit the tile floor. Walter was sure he was dead, but when he picked him up, he had no injuries nor did he cry. (Angel at work.) Another time, when the family was in Fort Myers, at the kitchen table, a ceiling fan was on and it fell on the table where Clay had been placed in his bassinet just minutes before. (Angel at work.) Another time, when Clay was about three years old and swimming at the club in Hartland pool. Walter was watching him and as he walked out on the diving board, he turned to say something to Walter and fell head first on the concrete. The sound of him hitting the concrete still lingers in his mind and Walter thought he was killed, but aside from a knot on his forehead, he was OK. He was taken to the emergency room and examined but found to be OK. (Angel at work.)

Pam and Walter found a swing and climbing set for sale nearby and moved it to the backyard for Clay. There were kids up and down the street and they all found their way to the Coxes backyard to play with Clay on the swings. The home became the center of attraction for the neighborhood. At times, there were five to ten kids playing in the backyard in or near the swing. When snow came, the backyard was a great place to slide down the hill to the street and the neighborhood children enjoyed every minute of it. Pam was so wonderful with all the children that they loved coming to the Cox house to play inside or outside. Pam is an angel for sure.

Walter was a broker of real estate, having taught real estate back in 1963 and received his broker license to give him additional credentials. He spent a lot of time working on selling and listing real estate, along with Pam, who had received and earned her sales license. In addition, he tried his hand at substitute teaching in the Fayette County Schools. One morning, while teaching at Edith Ewing Middle School, two boys, about ten years old, got into a fight. They were pounding each other with books, so Walter told all the kids to go get a big teacher to stop them. (The boys were as large as Walter.) The kids brought the football coach and he held both of them by their collars and stopped the fight. After that, Walter decided against being a subteacher. Pam kept busy with Clay and Walter stayed out of her hair. The entire family of three and Pam's mother, who stayed with them part of the year, traveled to Florida in the winter for three months, staying with the sisters. In the year 2000, Walter, Pam and Clay attended the reunion of the 70th infantry Association and for one of the entertainments, Clay sang the STAR SPANGELED BANNER BEFORE 600 ATTENDEES.

Clay age 5

When Clay finally grew to school age, he attended the preschool in Miami, where he made friends and loved the teachers. When Clay reached the age to go to kindergarten, the visits to

Clay

Florida became less frequent and Clay was enrolled at the Tates Creek Presbyterian Church School on Rapid Run Road, only a few blocks from home. He really liked the school and the teachers doted on him because he was so bright. When the time came for him to go to public school, Walter worked another angel miracle and Clay was accepted at Cassidy School. He started playing the violin in the small orchestra and displayed a talent for music. He could sing and did so every time he had an opportunity. His grades were perfect and again the teachers loved him.

Clay age 18 mos.

Clay & Walter Father's Day

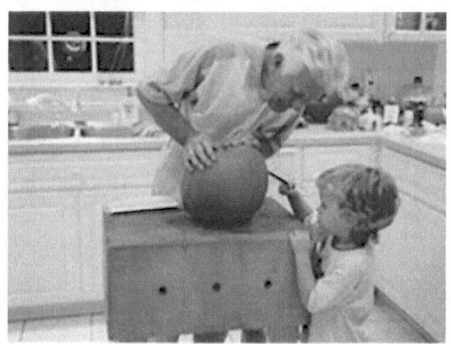

Halloween

Clay Walter & Pam

FT Myers - Beach

Beach Naples

Clay & Walter
Naples Fishing

Again, in the next progression to sixth, seventh and eighth grades at Morton, at first Clay started with a violin and piano and did very well. He also was good at singing and was in the choir at Calvary Baptist and sang in the school chorus. Later on Clay played trombone in the band and was in many of the extracurricular activities. When he reached the ninth grade and was going to his present school, Henry Clay High, he took two tests and his grades of 95 and 96 admitted him to the academy, which was the upper tier of only 85 students out of the 2,300. He has been in the jazz band, wind ensemble, the marching band and steel band and plays sports in the Henry Clay Lacrosse Team Club. He attends school at seven thirty each morning and usually stays until five or six o'clock. His grades were great! Clay is now six feet two inches tall and helped the director of the marching band in his junior and senior years. At an age (sixteen) when the world is yours and you have many friends, he is the organizer of the Disk Club and a six-man private band, which has performed several times in public. He plays the guitar, trombone, piano and sings.

Walter resigned from the Lexington Country Club in 1998 after the family moved to Hartland. Thereafter, he played golf with Bob Drake, Bob Loucks and many other golfers who had moved from the club. Walter was elected vice president of the club in 1997 and really hated to give it up, but being thirteen miles from the location was just too much driving for him, along with the fact that many of the members were retiring and leaving the membership.

Out of Retirement

During all this time, since his official retirement from the law firm in 1988, Walter was "of counsel" with his law firm and continued to practice law part time. In the year 2004, Walter decided Clay needed to have a father who was gainfully a full-time lawyer. He obtained a position with a company that let him practice law at his own pace and allow him to play golf at his leisure. In addition, Walter and Pam decided to help Teresa Isaac become mayor of Lexington. They attended the first fund-raiser for her and thereafter became a backer for her. They attended her first fund-raising party, took a platter of goodies to eat and then had a party at their house for her.

She won the election and became mayor and thereafter found a position for Walter in the administration. He only worked some three hours each day helping out in Social Services, calling on all the various divisions of the services. To him it appeared as if there were overlapping services throughout the system of the city. He reported this to Mayor Isaacs and was told to keep his ideas to himself. Thereafter, he became a public relations person. He called on three or more businesses in the city each and every day bringing them greetings from the mayor's office and asking them if they needed assistance in their business. After three years, he had spoken to 300 or more independent and corporate businesses and was received by all of them in a good spirit. The next election, Teresa lost to Jim Newberry and Walter was no longer needed.

The new law practice consists of preparing trusts, wills, powers of attorney, health powers of attorney and instructions for the trustees. During the next three years, he prepared over 350 trusts at the offices located at 2333 Alexandria Drive, Lexington, Kentucky. In working with the three or four persons contacting clients, delivering the trusts, he found a vocation different than he had been heretofore familiar with. Many of the clients phoned for instructions and changes and meeting with them to accomplish the purpose was very gratifying for him.

In 2007, a change took place in the employment and Walter decided to open his own law office and continue doing the same type of legal services.

After the office was opened at a different location on New Circle Road, Lexington, Kentucky, it stayed there for two years and then moved back to Alexandria Drive, where it was originally located. The offices were on the first floor compared with the previous one on the second floor, where clients had to use the elevator. Since 2007, he has prepared over 500 trusts and has received many phone calls and personal thanks for having done so.

His written advice has been read by many. His writings have appeared in a magazine called *Fifty Plus* and others. Walter is called upon to mediate, negotiate, arbitrate and counsel a large number of clients. During the years 2007 until 2010, Walter was an arbitrator to many cases referred to him. He had to read the complaint by the plaintiff and the answer filed by the defendant and make a finding and submit it to the arbitration company. It did not pay much money but was fun while it lasted. Many of his clients want him to practice other types of cases, but he limits himself to estate planning, wills, trusts and probate. Most of the practice is completing living trusts for clients to avoid probate. The people he counsels and prepares trusts for are a cross-section of the United States of America and particularly, Kentucky. Many are local to the Bluegrass area and others have migrated to Lexington and work or retire there. It is a stimulating practice in that every trust is different and needs personal attention. Many are friends, fellow church members, fellow Golfers, old clients from the old law firm (Fowler, Measle and Bell, formerly Fowler, Bell, Cox and Hancock, formerly Bell and Cox back in 1955-1956 and many more new clients have become trust clients of Walter.

In the practice, other problems of clients creep into the office and need help. Walter tries to accommodate everyone by representing them or sending them to the old law firm or other attorney specialties. The idea that Walter is happy doing what he does is represented by his continuing to work at his chosen life career. No one should ever retire, so says Walter and he backs it up with continuing to be a workaholic. Time and again, he tells the story that before FDR and 1934, no one retired because there was no retirement except money you earned and saved. The Social Security you know now was not in existence and was created when the life expectancy of the average man was under

The Law Offices of Walter C. Cox, Jr., & Associates, LLC

Walter C. Cox, Jr., Senior Attorney
Rated A V by Martindale (30 years)
2333 Alexandria Dr.
Lexington, Kentucky 40504-3215

Member BBB of Central KY
Member of Commerce Lexington
Admitted to Practice at U. S. SUPREME COURT
Title-Senior Counselor by the Kentucky Bar Association

Telephone 859/514-6033
Fax 859/514-6702
Email info@waltercoxlaw.com
Cell phone 859..318.4020

TIPS FOR LIVING TO BE 100 OR MORE

1. EAT VEGGIES, FRUIT, FISH, WHOLE GRAINS
2. DRINK PLENTY OF WATER
3. BATHE AT LEAST 3 TIMES WEEKLY
4. EXERCISE 30 MINUTES DAILY (WALK)
5. DO NOT WORRY AND PRAY OFTEN
6. PLAY OFTEN AND ENJOY
7. RELAX ALL OF YOUR TIME AT WORK OR PLAY
8. SLEEP WELL AT LEAST 8 HOURS A DAY
9. CHECK WITH A DOCTOR ONCE A YEAR
10. NEVER RETIRE (KEEP WORKING AT SOMETHING YOU ENJOY
11. WHEN DRIVING, KEEP YOUR EYES FOCUSED ON THE ROAD.
12. MAINTAIN OR RETURN TO THE WEIGHT YOU HAD AT AGE 18
13. BE MARRIED AND ENJOY YOUR PARTNER ONCE EACH WEEK
14. READ A BOOK EVERY MONTH AND READ NEWSPAPER DAILY
15. BELIEVE IN JESUS AND TRUST THAT HE WILL TAKE CARE OF YOU
16. BELONG TO GROUPS OF PEOPLE AND SOCIALIZE WITH THEM
17. AS YOU AGE FIND YOUNGER FRIENDS (THE OLDER ONES DIE)
18. DO NOT SIT IN SOFT CHAIRS (STAND A LOT AND MOVE OFTEN)
19. SEND LETTERS, THANK YOU NOTES, EMAILS, FAXES TO LOVED ONES
20. AND LAST BUT NOT LEAST (ENJOY A DRINK OF ALCOHOL EACH DAY.

BY: WALTER C. COX, JR

TRUSTS, ESTATES, WILLS, POWERS OF ATTORNEY & HEALTH POWERS OF ATTORNEY
54 years of experience, practicing Law, Speaking, writing and giving guidance.

sixty-five years, so if you worked and paid Social Security for twenty years and died before sixty-five, you received only $200 to bury your body. Therefore, the government made money for many years from Social Security and now that the normal man lives to age seventy-nine and the fact that the government did not save the money it collected from SS, it is going broke and needs fixing. What really ruined the retirement plan was the new facets of it such as disability. So many people claim they are disabled and draw SS long before they are sixty-five plus the longevity of men and women that it pays out more than it can possible take in from working people today.

Walter has written articles about the war, about life and health (see attached). He belongs to a group called Seventieth Infantry Association and attended all the meetings from 1977 until the last one in 2011. There were 900 or more attendees, when the association met in Lexington during the year 1980 and the last one held in 2011 had only eighty-five active war veterans attending. This year,2012 in October, the association will meet in New Orleans in October, but Walter will not attend. In 2014, the association will meet in Ft Wayne Indiana and there probably will be less than 85 attending.

In 2008, the 70th Division was reactivated at Fort Knox.

Walter was State of Ky coordinator and was ask by the President to attend and give a talk on the Division during War II. He, Pam and Clay went to Knox and spent the night before in the Officers quarters. The next morning after a breakfast with the General, Walter gave a 30 minute talk to all the new cadre for the Division Walter ask the General why he was not in dress uniform and the General apologized and replied that he could go

get dressed up for the occasion but did not actually do it. Walter's picture with the General appeared on the front page of the next Trailblazer magazine.

During the recent years, Walter has been the Kentucky coordinator and was vice president of the East during the years 1978-1980. He was awarded the Trailblazer award some ten years ago, which signifies a lot of work for the association. (Pic)

On Thursday September 13, 2012, he spoke to the Bluegrass Kiwanis Club here in Lexington. His subject was trusts, but he reminded the club that he had a plaque showing he had spoken to the club in 1976. Two or three of the members were also in World War II and were older than Walter and one of the members was the builder (F. C. Kindred) whom Walter bought a house from in 1954.

Religion

About ten years ago, Walter who had been a Baptist all his life, decided on his own to be crismated into the Greek Orthodox Church. At the time he decided, the family were visiting Miami with the Shaws. With Elpitha as his sponsor, he became orthodox.

As soon as he returned home, the congregation elected him to the council of the church. There he served for six years and then decided to resign and not run again. He then was appointed to be the stewardship chair for the church. He served the church and made many pleas for pledges from the members bringing in more money each year.

Walter and Pam entertain and enjoy lots of clients and friends. On birthdays, Christmas, Derby Day, Fourth of July, Halloween, Thanksgiving and other holidays, Pam cooks the Greek recipes that have been passed down from her mother and grandmother. To say the menu is good is no description of the cooking art. She makes baklava better than any other in the world. Her many types of dishes make the visitors ask for the recipes and some are given and some are hidden away from any outsiders.

One Christmas party was held in the condo on Maxwell and Upper streets, where they lived when first married. Everyone in the Greek Orthodox Church were invited, along with all their friends. It is estimated that over 200 attended. The president of the University of Kentucky, David Roselle, the mayor of the city, representatives, senators, ministers; golfers and half of the church parishioners were there. Pam's mother, Patricia, was there and although she could not speak English, she was included in everyone's conversation. Needless to say that party was a success and was one to remember.

Speaking of Pam's Mom, she was a bright, sturdy, hardworking lady who new almost everything about anything there was to know. She really knew how to treat a man. When Walter would come in at night and sit down on the couch, this lady would put his feet on a footstool and take off his shoes. Every night at the dinner table, she would lift her glass and say, "Yamas" (To your good health). She crossed herself and repeated a prayer every time she sat down to the table. She was the reason the family came to the United States and Walter thanked her for doing so.

Her cooking was passed down in the family by Elpitha Collis Shaw, who now uses most of the recipes for her wonderful cooking. Pam is running a close second but does not prepare as many of the Greek recipes as Elpitha. The entire family are good cooks and Pam's brother, Nick, is now becoming a gourmet cook. We now know why there was a Greek restaurant in every town in the twenties and thirties. All the Greek immigrants knew how to eat and to cook, so that is the way they made a living in America. As soon as they had children, they saw to it that they had a good education and specialty in some field and then the Greek cooks were no more. So now we have very few Greek restaurants and in fact, there are none in Lexington, Kentucky. Pam likes to prepare for a party and has a party for the Derby. Most years, there are forty or more guests and Pam has a pre-derby hors d'oeuvre; and at the finish of the race, she has a full dinner. They have betting, pools and mint juleps for the fun and camaraderie. She also has many parties for birthdays, New Year's Eve, Christmas, Fourth of July and sometimes just for Clay and his friends.

One night, just recently, when the snow was on the ground, Clay brought about fifteen boys over to the house to spend the night. They had a few girls with them also, but they were asked to leave at 11:00 p.m. The group of boys were very nondestructive and left without damaging anything in the basement.

Walter has his office at the 2333 Alexandria address, only on the first floor. Some of his clients think the entire building is occupied by his law firm because there are receptionists at the entrance and it looks as if there is only one occupant. It appears that way for all the tenants as each has a separate office up and down the hallways. Many of the tenants are now friends and clients of Walter and he has been invited to talk at lots of gatherings by stockbrokers and others. Walter just celebrated his eighty-ninth birthday on November 9, 2011 and Pam cooked a wonderful dinner for ten of his friends. In fact, when Walter was eighty-five, Pam had a cocktail party for about eighty of his friends, relatives and fellow golfers. Then on November 9, 2012, his 90th birthday was held at the Hartland Club. Relatives came from all over. Becky and family, Charlotte, Sarah, Kip flew from Danville, California. Pams sister Elpitha, husband Marty and son Martin IV drove from Miami.

(left to right, Pam, Becky, Charlotte, Walter, Clay and Sarah)
90th Birthday

Her nephews George Kokorelis and wife Ana and 2 daughters, George Titouris, Bill and Maria Kokorelis all came from Miami, Florida, Brother Nick Collis and wife, Noele, daughter, Vive Collis, son George Collis and Victoria his wife and Philip Collis. Nia Tsitouris and daughter Stefanie & son Bill all from Columbus Ohio Jean Tsiboukas, Clay's Godmother came from Tennessee.

There were a total of 80 more who were not relatives. Walter welcomed everyone and sang Thanks for the Memories to all.

Walter has been asked to speak at many organizations about trusts, including stockbrokers, University of Kentucky groups, churches, clubs and schools. Many times, someone will ask him what will happen to the client if Walter is finally unable to retain his law practice and service the clients. Lately, Walter replies that he is trying to outdo the World War I veteran who was championed last year (2011) as the last vet at age 114. They laugh and then he tells them that there will be a lawyer following him in his place and stead. However, it seems that many of his acquaintances, friends, relatives, attorneys, employees and others are dying and he goes to a funeral home weekly. Walter is now offering advice on living longer and enjoying it. He credits the fact that Pam feeds him healthy food, puts him to bed at the same time every night, keeps him in line on exercise and takes care of his sex life and that he has Clay to raise and educate. He tells everyone if he had not found Pam, he would have been in the cemetery long ago.

Life is good, with the old boy living in a home he and Pam designed and have improved during the past fifteen years. With a fully finished basement, tiled, with a large bath and with all his memorabilia on the walls, it is a haven for Clay and the teenagers. Walter, with his newly refinished bath, hot tub, tiles and new fixtures, feels like a king in a castle. Cody, the little maltipoo dog, keeps him walking and does his tricks daily. He now sleeps in the room with Walter and Pam and is a pleasure for both. He crawls or jumps into Walter's lap every time he sits down to watch TV. They advise the retirees to have a dog or cat, as it makes them healthy. Cody does that for Walter for sure.

Something new has been added to the Cox household. Norma Taylor bought a new 1987 Wagoneer Jeep when she lived in Washington DC. Around 1994, she took it to Fort Myers, where she and her father had a cottage at Rivers Edge Golf

Course. They used it when they visited the cottage and when Walter would visit his cottage, he would drive the jeep around and keep the battery up. On or about 2004, Norma bought a condo in Naples, Florida and decided she would sell the cottage in Fort Myers. She did not want to keep the jeep, so Walter flew to Florida, bought it from her and drove it to Lexington. For three years, Walter drove the jeep back and forth to his office and then Norma decided she needed it in Lexington because she had moved back and left her Lexus in Naples. Walter sold it to her and she kept it until just recently. Walter bought it back and then the idea was to give it to Clay to drive. After fixing the ding on the right front, repairing the transmission, new brakes, new shocks, new tires and checking all parts, it is running good. The next items that will take place is to paint the parts that need painting, fix the radio which has quit, fix the lights, check the engine for a tick and fix the tailgate so it will stay up. After all that and about $5,000 spent, it will be a good running Jeep. Clay will drive it to school and around town but not out of town. Clay has already posted his car on Facebook and is proud of it.

Recently, Clay had a little accident in the afternoon, turning from Alumni Drive onto Chinoe Drive, going North. He skidded into a Lexus and did scratch the left front fender but no damage to the Wagoneer. That night, however, while going to a birthday party, Clay got lost and ended up in Georgetown and hit a fireplug, which damaged the left front and headlights of the jeep. It is being repaired.

Speaking of the basement of their home, at a recent New Year's Eve party, which Pam put together in one day, Clay invited twenty kids his age to come to the party. Pam had about twenty adults, so the house was alive on New Year's Eve 2011 and 12. Nine of Clay's party were girls and the rest were boys. Nine of the boys spent the night and stayed until the afternoon of New Year's day. Incidentally, the Fayette County Board of Education named January 2 as the new day for school beginning after Christmas break. It should have been a holiday as celebrated by everyone in town except the school system. The courts, post office, offices and all were closed because the second fell on Sunday and the holiday followed the Sunday holiday. Walter wrote a letter to the editor and e-mailed the board about the error they made scheduling the return to school on an official holiday. Nothing has changed regarding the vacation time.

During the past year, 2011, the city of Lexington was charging $24 for senior golfers and it was limiting the number of golfers to almost half of what it had been in 2008 and 2009. Walter wrote a letter to the editor of the newspaper, telling them that the fees were too high and that they should lower them so more players would play. To Walter's surprise, the first game he played at the local Tates Creek Course, he found that the fee for eighteen holes for seniors was now $25 and that if you would pay $100 in advance, the fee would be only $18 for all 2012 at all Lexington golf courses. He paid that immediately because he will play more than twenty times this year.

The past year, 2010, Clay qualified for the State of Kentucky Jazz Competition, which was held in Louisville, Kentucky, at the main commerce building downtown. There were only twenty-six musicians who qualified from all over the state and with Clay being only a sophomore, he and one other boy were the youngest in the group. During that year, he also qualified for the district concert band and was first trombone.

Clay

This past year, 2011, he qualified for the State Concert Band and was one of the ten trombones from all over the state. Out of the group of Henry Clay High School students, he was one of only four who went to Louisville. The concert was held at the Art Center in Louisville, which was a beautiful place to listen to the beautiful music played by the band. Clay was also in the

Henry Clay High School marching band during the year and became one of the leaders of a division in the band. The band went to the state finals and finished at sixth place, which was the highest any Henry Clay band had ever finished. In 2013, Clay again qualified for the Stqte Jazz band but this time he was made LEAD TROMBONE. Again the trip to Louisville to witness the Jazz bank at the Galt house Hotel was a special event and with clay playing 2 solos, it was unforgettable.

Clay already has enough credits to be able to graduate, but he will finish his senior year at which time he will have college credits that will put him in his sophomore year at his choice of college. Clay is dating and a different girl every month. He is a member of a band of six (jazz), where he plays the guitar, trombone and sings. They just had three different nights of competition last week in April 2012 and won first place in each of the gigs among over fifteen competing bands. On February 28 the Henry Clay Jazz band played at the local COMEDY OFF BROADWAY. They were a hit of course and Clay played 3 solos during the exhibition. Recently the stars of Fayette County and Picture in uniform)

Resently many local Jazz bands from surrounding counties were invited to play at the Singletary center for the Arts. There were University of Kentucky Jazz band, another older mens band and the All Stars of the various high schools. Clay was invited as was his friends, Mo Patton and Jeff Doll. Walter told everyone that the high school band was the best.

Recently, on January 28, Walter drove downtown to Probate Court to file some pleadings. He parked on the side of the street opposite the District Court building. After watching all cars clear his path, he crossed Barr Street and about halfway across, an SUV backed up on the far side of the street and hit his left rear, knocking Walter to the blacktop. One second more and Walter would have been under the wheels of the vehicle. (Angel.)

He suffered a hit to the right cheek, shoulder, knees and knuckles on his hands. Many people soon gathered, including three police cars, ambulance and a nurse. They kept him on the pavement and blotted blood coming from his cheek and until the paramedic examined him would they let him get up. The man driving the SUV was an employee of IBM and was backing up to get to a parking space where someone was coming out. He obviously did not see Walter. He was nice and drove Walter to his doctor at South Clinic of UK. The doctor took one look at Walter and sent him to the St. Joseph Hospital emergency.

While there, they x-rayed his shoulder, took information about his insurance and finally, after an hour, left him in a room adjacent to the emergency room employees. The doctor he saw at the clinic provided an ice pack for the cheek. In the meantime, Pam, his wife, came to the emergency room and was with him. Walter asked an attendant for a drink of water and more ice. Finally, a doctor came and told him that his shoulder was not broken and he could be discharged. Never did anyone treat Walter or bring water or ice to him. He is recovering slowly and going to a chiropractor two times a week because his shoulder is painful when he reaches for anything. Now, after going to an orthopedic surgeon, he is going through therapy and his shoulder is gradually improving but he is continuing treatment at Kort chiropractor.

Walter is living a great life with his sexy wife, Pam and his eighteen-year-old senior high school son, Clay. With his son in marching band, it seems it is go to something all the time. Tryouts, competition, tests, girlfriends, visits by the boys in the jazz band and others take up a lot of time. It is wonderful and with Clay saying he is going to attend the University of Kentucky to be a doctor of medicine is very gratifying. Pam being active in the church, in school activities and keeping house keeps her busy, so she does not miss Walter going to work every day or playing golf whenever he can.

Many of the clients ask what they are going to do when he quits or dies. His reply is "What makes you think I am going to quit or die?"

This book will require a sequel and it most certainly will have one, if Walter continues to be taken care of by his "special angel." And is completely sure that God created his guardian Angel to protect him and keep him healthy and free from harm.

Credits: Without the help of his wife, Pam, his son Clay, his friend Ryan Messner, he could not have put this book together.

To all who have read this book.

May the Lord make the sun shine on your face and protect you from harm all the days of your life. May you have good health and happiness and pass it on to all you meet.

Writings of different times:

Things that Change Your Life

Becoming an Officer in the Service, Becoming a Married Man,

Having a Baby and Becoming an Attorney

How to Live To Be One Hundred

Tips to Live by and Be Healthy

The Forgotten Father

Pictures not related:

THE UNITED STATES OF AMERICA
TO ALL WHO SHALL SEE THESE PRESENTS, GREETING:
THIS IS TO CERTIFY THAT
THE PRESIDENT OF THE UNITED STATES OF AMERICA
AUTHORIZED BY EXECUTIVE ORDER, FEBRUARY 4, 1944
HAS AWARDED

THE BRONZE STAR MEDAL

TO

Captain Walter C. Cox, Jr., O 556 583, Infantry

FOR

MERITORIOUS ACHIEVEMENT
IN GROUND OPERATIONS AGAINST THE ENEMY
European Theater of Operations, 4 January 1945 - 7 January 1945
GIVEN UNDER MY HAND IN THE CITY OF WASHINGTON
THIS   15th   DAY OF   July   19 49

Charlotte and Sarah

Clay & Walter
Father's Day 2013

Clay's graduation picture Henry Clay High School 2013

Clay's graduation picture for 2013

www.ingramcontent.com/pod-product-compliance
Lightning Source LLC
Chambersburg PA
CBHW021440070526
44577CB00002B/230